Healing In The Astral Realms:

A Light Workers Guide to Astral Projection & Energetic Healing

By: Shani Riviere

Table of Contents

Chapter 1

Introduction

Astral projection is the process of consciously leaving your physical body to explore other dimensions and planes of existence. This practice is also known as an out-of-body experience (OBE), where your consciousness—often referred to as your "astral body"—separates from the physical self while remaining tethered by a subtle energetic cord. During an astral journey, your astral body can travel through different realms, access information, and interact with beings of light, spirit guides, or even loved ones who have passed on.

Astral projection is not limited to time or space; the dimensions you access through this practice can allow you to explore past lives, alternate realities, or even future events. This capacity to traverse beyond the physical can be a powerful tool for healing, particularly for light workers and medical intuitives who need to access deeper layers of consciousness and energy fields for transformative healing work.

The Role of a Light Worker and Medical Intuitive in Healing

As a light worker, your purpose is to channel healing energy, raise vibrational frequencies, and facilitate the spiritual, emotional, and physical healing of others. You work as a bridge between the spiritual and material worlds, using your intuitive gifts to guide others on their healing journeys. Astral projection allows you to extend your reach beyond the limitations of the physical world, enabling you to perform energetic healing at a much deeper and more profound level.

Medical intuitives use their heightened perception to detect imbalances within a person's body and energy field. They can sense illness, blockages, and trauma in the physical and energetic bodies. Through astral projection, medical intuitives can explore subtle realms where these imbalances originate, helping to facilitate holistic healing that transcends the purely physical.

Both light workers and medical intuitives can use astral projection as a tool to access a higher level of wisdom, work with guides in the astral realms, and access healing modalities that are not always available in the physical world. Whether diagnosing energy imbalances or transmitting healing light, the ability to travel astrally can accelerate your healing work and amplify your intuitive powers.

Why Astral Healing?

Healing is not just about the body—it's about the mind, emotions, and spirit. Many illnesses and emotional imbalances are rooted in the energetic and spiritual planes, where blockages or unresolved trauma reside. Traditional healing methods often focus on addressing symptoms on the physical level, but they do not always resolve the underlying causes. Astral healing allows light workers and medical intuitives to bypass the physical realm and work directly with the soul and energy body, the true origin of most ailments.

When you astral project, you can:

- Access realms of pure healing energy.
- Connect with spiritual guides and ascended beings who assist in healing.
- Discover and heal energetic imbalances or past life trauma.
- Retrieve soul fragments lost due to trauma or spiritual disconnection.

Astral healing also provides you with an expanded perspective on the interconnectedness of mind, body, and spirit. By working in these higher planes, you not only heal individuals but also contribute to the healing of the collective consciousness, as well as the Earth's energy grid.

This book will focus on techniques and practices to help guide healers on how to integrate astral projection into their healing work.

Chapter Two: Preparing for Astral Projection

Astral projection requires a combination of physical relaxation, mental focus, and energetic readiness. Proper preparation is key to ensuring a smooth and positive experience in the astral realm. In this chapter, we'll cover how to create the right environment, cleanse and protect your energy, and prepare your mind and body for the astral journey.

Creating a Sacred Space for Practice

The environment around you is a reflection of your internal state. A cluttered or chaotic space can distract you during your astral work. To set the stage for astral projection, you need a space that feels safe, comfortable, and energetically clear. Here's how to create a sacred space that supports your astral travel:

Instructions:

1. **Select a Quiet Location**: Choose a room where you won't be disturbed. It should be a space that you associate with peace, relaxation, and introspection. Bedrooms, meditation spaces, or quiet corners work well. The space should be free from distractions, such as loud noises, bright lights, or electronic devices that could interrupt your experience.

2. **Cleanse the Energy**: It's essential to clear the room of any lingering negative or stagnant energy. Smudging the room with sage, palo santo, or incense can purify the environment. To do this, light the smudge stick or incense, and walk clockwise around the room, holding the intention that any lower vibrational energies are being cleared. You can say a mantra like, "I cleanse this space of any negative energies and invite only light and love to remain."

3. **Set Up Sacred Objects**: Enhance the energy of the room by placing objects that raise its vibrational frequency. This can include crystals (such as clear quartz, amethyst, or selenite), candles, spiritual symbols (like the Flower of Life or mandalas), or personal items that hold spiritual significance for you. Arrange these objects on an altar or around the room in a way that feels intuitive to you.

4. **Lighting**: Soft, warm lighting helps create a calm atmosphere. Use candles, salt lamps, or dimmable lights to provide a gentle glow. Too much light can be overstimulating, while complete darkness might make you feel uneasy. Aim for a balance that feels comforting.

5. **Optional: Sound**: You can add a layer of auditory support by playing soft meditative music, nature sounds, or binaural beats that are designed for relaxation or astral projection. Choose sounds that relax you and deepen your focus.

Pro Tip: Once you've created your sacred space, use it consistently for your astral projection practice. Over time, your body and mind will associate this space with relaxation and spiritual work, making it easier to slip into the proper state for astral travel.

Grounding and Centering Techniques

Grounding and centering are vital parts of preparation for astral projection. These practices help you anchor your energy, ensuring that while your consciousness explores the astral realms, you remain tethered to your physical body and the Earth. Grounding also helps prevent feelings of disorientation when you return from your astral travels.

Grounding Visualization:

1. **Sit Comfortably**: Sit on a chair or directly on the ground with your feet flat on the floor. You may also lay down if you prefer.

2. **Visualize Roots**: Close your eyes and take a few deep breaths. As you exhale, imagine roots growing from the base of your spine (your root chakra) or the soles of your feet. See these roots pushing down through the floor and deep into the Earth's core.

3. **Connect to the Earth's Energy**: As your roots reach the Earth's core, visualize them anchoring into its molten center. Now, imagine the Earth's grounding, stabilizing energy flowing up through the roots and into your body. Feel this energy infusing your legs, your spine, and your entire body with a sense of stability and safety.

4. **Release Energy**: As the Earth's energy rises into your body, visualize any stress, tension, or negative energy being pulled down through your roots and absorbed by the Earth. The Earth neutralizes these energies, leaving you feeling lighter and more grounded.

Centering Technique:

1. **Take Some Time to Focus on Your Breath**: Close your eyes and then take slow, deep breaths. Inhale deeply into

your abdomen, feeling your stomach rise, and then exhale slowly, feeling your body relax more with each breath.

2. **Bring Your Awareness Inward**: Focus your attention on your center, which can be your heart space or solar plexus. Imagine a small point of light or energy at this center.

3. **Expand the Light**: With each inhale, visualize this point of light expanding, growing brighter and larger. With each exhale, feel the light radiating outward, filling your entire body and stabilizing your energy field.

4. **Find Your Inner Stillness**: Stay focused on this light and the sensation of calm that it brings. Let any external thoughts, worries, or distractions fade away as you center yourself in this inner stillness.

Daily Energy Hygiene: Cleansing Your Aura

Your aura is the energetic constantly shifting and and changing field that surrounds and protects your body. It's essential to keep your aura clear of negative energies or attachments, especially when preparing for astral projection, as a clean aura makes it easier to access higher vibrational realms.

White Light Cleansing:

1. **Find a Comfortable Position**: Sit or lie down in a comfortable position in your sacred space.

2. **Visualize White Light**: Close your eyes and visualize a brilliant, pure white or golden light above your head. This light represents divine energy, radiating love and healing.

3. **Cleansing Process**: Imagine this light slowly descending and enveloping your entire body. See it cleansing and purifying your aura, dissolving any dark spots, stagnant energy, or attachments. Allow this light to wash over you, leaving your energy field clear and radiant.

4. **Seal Your Aura**: After the cleansing, visualize the light forming a protective shield around you, keeping your energy field pure and safe.

Salt Baths for Energy Clearing:

1. **Prepare Your Bath**: Fill a bathtub with warm water and add 1-2 cups of Epsom salts or Himalayan salt. You can also add essential oils like lavender or frankincense for added relaxation.

2. **Set Your Intention**: Before entering the bath, set the intention to cleanse and recharge your aura. You can say something like, "I now release any and all negative or stagnant energies and welcome only peace and light into my being."

3. **Soak and Relax**: Soak in the bath for at least 20 minutes, visualizing the water drawing out any negative energy and impurities from your aura. As you soak, feel yourself becoming lighter and more energized.

Smudging Your Aura:

1. **Choose Your Tool**: Use sage, palo santo, or incense for this practice. Light the smudge stick or incense and let the smoke rise.

2. **Cleanse Your Aura**: Pass the smoke over your body, starting at your head and moving downward to your feet. As the smoke surrounds you, visualize it clearing any negative or heavy energies from your aura.

Strengthening Your Connection to Source

Astral projection often involves working with higher planes of consciousness and connecting with divine energies. Strengthening your connection to Source energy will help guide and protect you during your astral journeys.

Meditation to Strengthen Connection:

1. **Sit in Stillness**: Sit comfortably in your sacred space, close your eyes, and begin by focusing on your breath.

2. **Visualize Source**: Picture a bright light high above your head, representing Source, the Divine, or the Universe. This light is infinite, loving, and connected to all things.

3. **Receive Light**: Imagine this light beaming down into the top of your head (your crown chakra) and flowing through your entire body. Feel the divine energy filling you with peace, love, and protection.

4. **Gratitude Practice**: Once you feel connected, take a moment to express gratitude for this divine connection. Feel the deep sense of trust and safety that comes from being connected to Source.

Nature Connection:

1. **Spend Time Outdoors**: Nature is one of the easiest and most effective ways to strengthen your connection to Source. Walk barefoot on the grass, sit by a tree, or meditate near a body of water.

2. **Mindful Nature Walks**: As you walk, focus on the sights, sounds, and smells around you. Really feel the earth under your feet. Feel the breeze on your skin and let yourself feel connected to the natural world as a reflection of the divine.

3. **Grounding Through Nature**: If you feel disconnected, simply spend time outside in nature, allowing your body and energy to realign with the natural rhythms of the Earth.

Meditation and Visualization Techniques

Meditation and visualization are essential tools for astral projection. Regular practice helps quiet the mind, relax the body, and prime your consciousness for the transition into the astral plane.

Progressive Relaxation for Astral Travel:

1. **Get Comfortable:** Lie down in your sacred space, arms by your side, and close your eyes.

2. **Focus on Your Toes:** Bring your attention to your toes. Consciously relax them, then move up to your feet, calves, thighs, abdomen, chest, arms, and head. With each body part, focus on releasing any tension.

3. **Deep Breathing:** After your body is relaxed, focus on your breath. Inhale deeply for four counts through your nose and exhale slowly for four counts. Repeat this until your mind is calm and focused.

Visualization to Aid Astral Projection:

1. **Visualize Floating**: After you've relaxed your body and calmed your mind, visualize yourself gently floating above your physical body. See your astral body separating and drifting upwards.

2. **Create an Astral Landscape**: Visualize yourself entering a peaceful landscape—perhaps a beach, a forest, or a temple. This landscape is your entry point to the astral realm. Spend time visualizing the details of this place and feeling its energy.

3. **Allow Yourself to Transition**: As your visualization deepens, allow your consciousness to transition fully into this astral space. Stay relaxed and trust the process.

Pro Tips for Successful Preparation:

Consistency: The more regularly you practice these techniques, the easier it becomes to relax, ground, and enter the astral realm.

- **Journaling**: Keep a journal of your preparation process, writing down what works for you and noting how you feel before and after each attempt. This will help you refine your technique.

- **Set Clear Intentions**: Before each astral projection session, clearly state your intention, whether it's for healing, guidance, or exploration. This will help direct your journey and ensure you receive the insights or healing you seek.

Chapter Three: Steps to Achieve Astral Projection

Achieving astral projection involves entering a deeply relaxed state, separating your consciousness from your physical body, and navigating through the astral plane. This process can take time and practice, so it's important to remain patient, consistent, and open to different techniques. In this chapter, we'll explore common methods of astral projection, how to achieve deep relaxation, how to recognize the signs that you're transitioning to the astral plane, and tips for first-time travelers.

Overview of Common Methods

There are several techniques for achieving astral projection, and each person may resonate with a different method. Below are some of the most popular and effective techniques for inducing astral projection.

The Rope Technique

The Rope Technique is one of the most well-known methods for astral projection. It's simple, effective, and can be done by anyone with consistent practice. This technique involves visualizing a strong sturdy rope hanging above your body while lying down in a relaxed state. You will imagine reaching up and pulling the rope, using your mental strength and focus to "climb" out of your physical form. As the mental visualization deepens, yo may feel subtle shifts in your body such as vibrations or a floating sensation. By maintaining focus on the act of pulling yourself upward, you can eventually experience and out-of-body experience (OBE), achieving astral projection. They key is to remain calm and centered, allowing your astral body to move freely without tension or fear.

Instructions:

4. **Lie Down in a Comfortable Position**: Find a quiet, comfortable space. Lie flat on your back with your arms at your sides and close your eyes. You will want to make sure that your body is fully relaxed.

5. **Achieve Deep Relaxation**: Before beginning, use deep breathing or progressive relaxation techniques (covered in Chapter Two) to reach a deep state of relaxation. Your mind should be calm and your body should feel heavy.

6. **Visualize the Rope**: In your mind's eye, imagine a strong, sturdy rope hanging above you, extending from the ceiling or sky. The rope is within arm's reach.

7. **Begin Climbing the Rope**: Visualize your astral body (not your physical body) reaching out and grasping the rope. Slowly, begin pulling yourself up the rope. You might feel your body getting lighter or a pulling sensation as you climb higher.

8. **Separate from Your Body**: Continue climbing the rope in your mind, feeling yourself lifting higher and further away from your physical body. Eventually, you will feel a distinct shift as your astral body detaches from your physical form.

9. **Explore the Astral Plane**: Once you've separated, take a moment to stabilize yourself in the astral realm. Look around and acclimate yourself to the new surroundings before proceeding.

The Roll-Out Technique

The Roll-Out Technique works well for those who prefer movement-based visualization. It is one of the most well-known and effective methods for initiating astral projection. It involves using the sensation of movement to facilitate the separation of your astral body from your physical body. This technique focuses on using subtle, yet deliberate, movements to "roll" out of your body, mimicking the sensation of physically turning or rolling over, while keeping the physical body completely still and relaxed.

How the Roll-out Technique Works

1. **Deep Relaxation and Preparation**: To start, you need to be in a deeply relaxed, meditative state. Achieving this state is critical, as it allows your body to be at rest while your consciousness remains alert. It may help to lie down, flat on your back, in a comfortable position, in a quiet space. Use progressive muscle relaxation, breathwork, or meditation to help your body achieve a calm, peaceful state.

2. **Entering the Hypnagogic State**: Relax your body completely. You should feel as though your body is melting into the bed or floor. Focus on your breathing and allow yourself to drift further into a relaxed, meditative state. As you approach the hypnagogic state (the transitional phase between wakefulness and sleep), your mind should remain focused while your body becomes increasingly detached from physical sensations. This is the point where you are conscious but on the verge of sleep—a key moment for astral projection.

3. **Visualize the Roll-out Motion**: Once you are fully relaxed and in the right state of mind, visualize yourself gently rolling to the side, as if you were rolling out of bed. Visualize your astral body rolling out of your physical body. You are physically turning onto your side, or rolling forward or backward, without actually moving your physical body. Focus on the sensation of rolling out, creating a strong mental image of your astral body separating from your physical body as your physical body remains still.

4. **Feel the Separation**: As you visualize the rolling motion, start to engage your sense of movement. Focus on the sensation of your astral body shifting out of alignment with your physical form. Many people experience a moment of subtle vibrations, a light tugging sensation, or a floating feeling as the astral body begins to separate.

5. **Exit the Body**: Once you feel the shift, continue the motion until you are fully out of your physical body. This could be accompanied by a sense of lightness or floating. Remain calm and composed as you become aware of your astral surroundings. Take a moment to steady yourself, then begin exploring the astral realm.

Key Tips for Success

- **Patience and Practice**: Like all astral projection techniques, the Roll-out Technique requires patience and consistent practice. Don't be discouraged if it doesn't happen immediately. Each attempt strengthens your ability to project.

- **Stay Calm**: It's essential to remain calm throughout the process. Excitement or fear can pull you back into your physical body and end the projection prematurely. Stay focused on the feeling of separation and maintain a relaxed mindset.

- **Focus on Sensations**: Engaging your sense of movement is crucial. Rather than purely visualizing, try to *feel* the rolling motion. The more realistic the sensation, the easier it will be for your astral body to separate.

By mastering the Roll-out Technique, you can consistently initiate astral projection, allowing for deeper exploration of the astral realm and its healing potential.

The Visualized Elevator Method

The Visualized Elevator Method is a powerful astral projection technique that uses the imagery and sensation of ascending or descending in an elevator to facilitate the separation of the astral body from the physical body. This method works particularly well because the mind responds strongly to the sensation of vertical movement, which can help trigger the release of the astral body. The elevator imagery is simple yet effective, providing a familiar and easily accessible mental construct that guides your consciousness through the process of projection. By visualizing yourself inside an elevator moving upwards or downwards, you create a sense of detachment from the physical body, making it easier for the astral body to separate. This technique also encourages a feeling of control, allowing you to direct your movement as you explore the astral realm.This method is helpful for those who prefer imagery related to upward movement, such as elevators, escalators, or floating upwards.

Instructions:

1. **Lie Down and Relax**: Begin by finding a quiet, comfortable space where you won't be disturbed. Lie flat on your back in a relaxed position and close your eyes. Use deep breathing techniques to calm your mind and body. Focus on breath and allow your muscles to relax and your mind to enter a peaceful, meditative state. It is essential to achieve deep physical relaxation so that your body remains still while your conciousness stays active.

2. **Visualize an Elevator**: Once you're deeply relaxed, imagine that you're standing in an elevator. Picture every detail: the doors, the buttons, and the walls of the elevator. You want to create a vivid mental image of the environment. This visualization should feel vivid and real to you.

3. **Press the Button**: In your mind, press the button for the top floor (or a number that symbolizes ascension for you). As the elevator begins to ascend, imagine yourself feeling lighter and more detached from your physical body.

4. **Feel the Rise**: As the elevator moves upwards, focus on the sensation of your astral body lifting higher and higher. You may feel a sense of weightlessness or floating as you rise.

5. **Exit the Elevator**: When you feel ready, imagine the elevator doors opening. Step out into the astral plane, leaving your physical body behind. Take a moment to orient yourself and explore the surroundings. Use this time to interact with spirit guides, visit healing spaces, or explore higher dimensions. Move through the realm with a sense of purpose always remaining calm and in control over your movements.

Key Tips for Success

- **Maintain Focus**: It's important to stay focused on the sensation of vertical movement. Distractions can bring you back to the physical body, so remain engaged with the feeling of rising or descending.

- **Patience is Crucial**: Like all astral projection techniques, the Visualized Elevator Method requires practice. Don't worry if separation doesn't occur on your first attempt. Each practice strengthens your connection to the astral realm.

- **Stay Calm During Exit**: When you feel the separation, stay calm and don't rush. Excitement or fear can bring you back to your body. Instead, take slow, deliberate steps as you exit the elevator into the astral realm.

With time and consistent practice, the Visualized Elevator Method can become a reliable tool for astral projection, helping you explore the spiritual dimensions and engage in deep healing work.

How to Achieve Deep Relaxation

Deep relaxation is the foundation of successful astral projection. Without fully relaxing your body and mind, your consciousness will remain anchored to your physical form. Here are some specific techniques for achieving the level of relaxation needed for astral projection:

Progressive Muscle Relaxation:

Instructions:

1. **Start at Your Feet:** Close your eyes and focus on your toes. Tense the muscles in your toes for a count of five, then release the tension and relax them completely. Move to your feet, calves, thighs, and so on.

2. **Move Up the Body:** Continue this process, tensing and relaxing each muscle group as you move up your body, from your legs to your abdomen, chest, arms, neck, and head.

3. **Breathe Deeply:** With each muscle group you relax, take deep, slow breaths. Inhale through your nose deeply, and exhale slowly through your mouth. With each exhale, let go of more tension.

4. **Enter a Meditative State:** Once your entire body feels relaxed, focus on your breath and let your mind drift into a meditative state. If thoughts arise, simply observe them without attachment, and allow them to pass.

Breath Counting Technique:

Instructions:

1. **Lie Comfortably**: Lie down and close your eyes, placing your hands on your abdomen.

2. **Focus on Your Breath**: Breathe in deeply through your nose, feeling your abdomen rise as you inhale. While exhaling slowly through your mouth, feel your abdomen fall.

3. **Begin Counting**: With each exhale, count your breaths. Start at one and work your way up to ten. After reaching

ten, start over at one. Focus only on the counting and the sensation of your breath.

4. **Let Go of Thoughts**: If your mind wanders, gently bring your attention back to your breath and the counting. Continue until your mind is calm, and your body is deeply relaxed.

Body Scan Relaxation:

Instructions:

1. **Lie Down:** Lie flat on your back with your arms at your sides. Close your eyes. Now take a few deep breaths to center yourself.

2. **Scan Your Body:** Starting from your toes, slowly bring your awareness to each part of your body. As you focus on each area (toes, feet, legs, hips, abdomen, etc.), consciously relax those muscles.

3. **Release Tension:** As you scan, imagine tension melting away from each body part. Visualize a wave of relaxation moving upward from your feet to your head, leaving your body feeling heavy and deeply relaxed.

4. **Stay Present:** Focus only on the present moment and the sensations in your body. Stay here until you feel completely relaxed.

Transition from the Physical to the Astral Plane

Once you've reached a deep state of relaxation, you may begin to notice signs that your consciousness is ready to transition to the astral plane. These sensations may feel strange at first, but they are natural and signal that you are close to separating from your physical body.

Common Sensations During the Transition:

1. **Vibrations or Tingling**: Many people report feeling vibrations or tingling in their body just before astral projection. This can feel like a buzzing or electrical current running through your body.

2. **Floating Sensation**: You might feel like you are floating above your bed or being pulled upward by an invisible force. This is a sign that your astral body is beginning to lift out of your physical body.

3. **Heaviness or Paralysis**: Some people experience a sensation of heaviness or temporary paralysis, also known as sleep paralysis. This can feel unnerving, but it is a natural part of the process as your consciousness detaches from your body.

4. **Humming or Rushing Sound**: You may hear a loud buzzing or rushing sound in your ears as your astral body begins to separate. This sound is common during the transition phase and should not be feared.

How to Handle the Transition:

The transition from the physical plane to the astral plane is a delicate and often subtle process that requires both mental focus and emotional control. This transition involves shifting your consciousness away from the physical body while remaining aware and grounded in your experience. Below are some key tips and strategies for handling this transition smoothly:

- **Stay Calm**: As you begin to experience signs of astral separation—such as vibrations, tingling, or floating sensations—it's essential to remain calm. Excitement, fear, or anxiety can quickly pull you back into your physical body. Focus on maintaining a state of calm awareness, knowing that this is a natural part of the process. Use deep, steady breathing to keep your mind relaxed and centered.

Tip: If you feel nervous, remind yourself that you are safe and protected. Visualize a shield of white or golden light around you to reinforce your sense of security.

Embrace the Sensations

During the transition, you may encounter unusual sensations, such as buzzing or vibrating throughout your body, a feeling of lightness or floating, or even auditory sounds like humming or ringing. These sensations are normal and indicate that your astral body is preparing to separate from the physical.

- **Tip**: Instead of resisting these sensations, lean into them. Acknowledge that they are part of the process, and allow yourself to relax deeper into the experience. The more you accept these sensations, the easier the transition becomes.

- **Focus on Your Intent**: As you feel these sensations, stay focused on your intent to separate from your physical body. Visualize yourself lifting up, floating, or moving out

Focus on Movement

Many astral projection techniques involve a feeling of movement whether it's rolling out, floating up, or falling down. As you approach the moment of separation, concentrate on this sense of movement. This helps shift your focus away from the physical body and solidifies the transition into the astral realm.

Tip: Whether you are using the Roll-out Technique, the Visualized Elevator Method, or another approach, stay focused on the mental imagery and sensations of moving. Keep your attention fixed on the feeling of rising, rolling, or floating until you fully transition into the astral plane.

- **Let Go of Control**: Once you feel the separation beginning, allow the process to happen naturally. Don't try to force the separation. Trust that your astral body knows what to do.

Tips for First-Time Travelers

Astral projection can feel overwhelming for first-time travelers, especially when dealing with unfamiliar sensations. These tips will help ease your journey and make your first astral projection experience smoother and more enjoyable.

Remain Patient:

Astral projection can take time and practice. Don't become discouraged if you don't succeed on your first few attempts. Every effort you make strengthens your ability to project, even if it feels like you aren't making progress.

Use Affirmations:

Repeating positive affirmations can help you stay calm and focused. Try saying, "I am safe and protected," or "I am ready to explore the astral plane with love and light" before and during your practice.

Stay Grounded:

Before beginning your astral projection, perform a grounding exercise (see Chapter Two) to keep yourself connected to your physical body and the Earth. This will help you feel more stable during your journey.

While it may seem counterintuitive, staying mentally grounded helps the transition. This means remaining aware of the process without overthinking or worrying about what's happening to your physical body. Keep your focus on the present moment, letting your awareness guide the transition naturally.

- **Tip**: Use a mantra or affirmation to keep your mind focused. Something simple like "I am safe, and I am in control" can anchor your awareness during the shift from the physical to the astral.

Trust the Process

The transition to the astral plane is often gradual, but it can also happen rapidly once separation begins. Trust in your ability to navigate this experience. The more relaxed and open you are to the process, the easier the transition will become. Trust that your guides, higher self, or spiritual helpers are there to support you.

- **Tip**: If at any point you feel uncertain or disoriented, ask your guides for assistance or set the intention to remain safe and focused. The astral realm responds strongly to your thoughts and intentions, so staying positive and confident is crucial.

By following these strategies, you can handle the transition from the physical plane to the astral plane with greater ease and confidence. The key is to remain calm, focused, and open to the experience while trusting in your ability to safely explore the astral realm. With practice, the transition will become smoother, allowing you to experience the full potential of astral healing and exploration.

Keep a Journal:

After each astral projection attempt, write down everything you experienced—whether you successfully projected or not. Keeping a journal will help you track your progress and refine your technique.

Expect Unusual Sensations:

Some sensations, such as vibrations, sounds, or temporary paralysis, can be startling. Remember that these sensations are normal and part of the process. Accept them as indicators that you're on the right track.

Return to Your Body Gently:

When you're ready to return from the astral plane, focus on your physical body and visualize your astral body merging back with it. Wiggle your fingers and toes, and take deep breaths to ground yourself.

Chapter Four: Navigating the Astral Realm for Healing

Once you've successfully projected into the astral plane, the next step is to learn how to navigate it with purpose. As a light worker or medical intuitive, you'll use the astral plane to connect with higher beings, healing energy centers, and guides who can assist in your work. In this chapter, you will learn how to recognize key aspects of the astral realm, how to connect with beings of light, and how to channel healing energy for yourself and others. We will also explore how to access and heal past life trauma during your astral journeys.

Identifying Healing Guides and Beings of Light

The astral realm is filled with various entities, ranging from beings of light (such as spirit guides, angels, and ascended masters) to more neutral or lower vibrational entities. As a healer, it's crucial to recognize and connect with beings who operate in high vibrational frequencies, as these beings can assist you in your healing work.

How to Call Upon Healing Guides

1. **Set an Intention Before You Begin**: Before you embark on your astral journey, set a clear intention to meet your spiritual guides or beings of light who can assist you in your healing work. You might say, "At this time I invite my highest vibrational guides and beings of light to assist me on this journey," or "I invite guides of healing who can help me bring love and light to myself and others."

2. **Relax and Open Your Energy Field**: Once you are in the astral realm, allow yourself to relax and open your energy field. This is crucial because guides and beings of light often communicate en-

ergetically, and being open helps you receive their messages.

3. **Ask for a Guide to Appear**: Once you feel grounded in the astral plane, mentally or verbally ask for a guide or being of light to reveal themselves. You can say, "I am open to meeting my healing guides. Please show yourself if you are here to help me in my healing work."

4. **Recognize Their Presence**: Beings of light can appear in various forms. Some may look like human figures surrounded by light, others may appear as shimmering energy, or you may simply sense their presence through feeling, intuition, or inner knowing. You might also hear guidance in the form of telepathic messages.

5. **Confirm the Vibrational Frequency**: To ensure you are connecting with a high-vibrational being, ask internally, "Are you of the highest light and here for my highest good?" A being of light will respond affirmatively, and you will feel a sense of peace, love, and safety. If you feel any discomfort or unease, simply ask them to leave or shield yourself with white light (refer to the protection techniques in Chapter Seven).

6. **Ask for Guidance or Healing**: Once you've connected with a healing guide, you can ask them for specific guidance or assistance with healing. They may give you insights into your energetic imbalances or those of your clients, or they may assist in clearing energetic blockages directly.

How to Build a Relationship with Your Guides

- **Consistency**: Regularly connect with your guides in the astral realm. The more you interact with them, the stronger your relationship will become. They will become more attuned to your energy, and you will find it easier to communicate with them.

- **Gratitude and Respect**: Always show gratitude for the guidance and assistance your astral guides provide. This strengthens your bond and helps you maintain a respectful, high-vibrational connection.

- **Journaling Your Encounters**: After each astral journey, journal your experiences with your guides. Note any messages, symbols, or insights they provided. Over time, you'll notice patterns and deeper guidance.

Understanding Energy Grids and Healing Centers in the Astral World

Understanding Energy Grids and Healing Centers in the Astral World is essential for those seeking to deepen their astral healing practice. In the astral realm, energy grids are intricate networks of high-frequency energy that flow through and around various dimensions, connecting different points of power and light. These grids serve as conduits for universal energy and act as frameworks for the balance and flow of life force across realms.

Within these grids, there are Healing Centers, which are specific locations or sacred spaces designed to facilitate deep spiritual and energetic healing. These centers are often overseen by ascended beings, spiritual guides, or angelic presences who work with advanced frequencies to restore balance, remove energetic blockages, and rejuvenate the soul. By visiting these healing centers in the astral realm, practitioners can receive powerful healing for physical, emotional, and spiritual issues, and also learn advanced techniques to bring back into their physical healing practices. Understanding and interacting with these energy grids and healing centers allows astral travelers to harness higher-dimensional energies for personal transformation and service to others, tapping into a vast reservoir of healing that transcends the limitations of the physical world.

These spaces are often frequented by beings of light, guides, and ascended masters. Visiting these areas can enhance your healing abilities, replenish your energy, or provide you with new healing techniques.

How to Find Energy Grids and Healing Centers

1. **Set the Intention**: Before projecting, set the intention to visit an astral healing center or energy grid. You can say, "I ask to be guided to an astral healing center that aligns with my highest good."

2. **Follow Your Intuition**: Once in the astral realm, trust your intuition to guide you. You may feel drawn to a particular direction, or a guide might appear to lead you to a healing center. The energy in these spaces is usually very high-vibrational and feels peaceful and expansive.

3. **Look for Key Signs**: Healing centers in the astral realm can appear as sacred temples, glowing light-filled spaces, or energy vortices. You may notice an increase in vibrational frequency as you approach, or you may see vivid colors, geometric patterns, or feel a sense of calm and serenity.

4. **Enter with Reverence**: As you enter these spaces, approach with reverence and respect. These centers are places of healing, and being in the right frame of mind will help you receive the energy

available there.

How to Work with Energy Grids and Healing Centers

1. **Receive Healing**: Once in the healing center, you can lie down, sit, or simply allow the energy to flow through you. Visualize the high-vibrational light surrounding you, infusing every part of your body and energy field with healing energy. Let this energy cleanse and rejuvenate your entire being.

2. **Ask for Specific Healing**: You can ask the healing energy in the center to work on specific areas of your body, mind, or spirit. If you are healing for someone else, focus on their energy and visualize them receiving the healing light.

3. **Learn New Healing Modalities**: Some astral healing centers offer teaching and initiation in higher-level healing techniques. You may be guided to specific healing tools, symbols, or light frequencies that you can use in your healing practice on the physical plane.

4. **Thank the Energies**: Before leaving, thank the healing center and the beings present for their support and healing energy. Always close your experience with gratitude and respect.

Techniques for Channeling Healing Energy from the Astral Plane to the Physical Plane

The astral plane offers access to powerful healing energy that can be channeled into your physical or energy body. You can also direct this energy towards others for healing. The following techniques will help you channel this energy effectively.

How to Channel Healing Energy for Yourself

1. **Visualize a Healing Light Source**: Once in the astral realm, visualize a powerful source of healing light—this may come from a guide, a healing center, or directly from Source energy. This light should be pure, high-vibrational, and filled with love.

2. **Draw the Light into Your Body**: Imagine this healing light flowing into your astral body. Focus on any areas where you feel tension, discomfort, or energetic blockages. Visualize the light dissolving the blockages and filling those areas with vibrant, restorative energy.

3. **Absorb the Healing Energy**: As the light continues to flow, let it fill every part of your being. Imagine it infusing your mental, emotional, and physical bodies, clearing out any negative or stagnant energy. As you breathe, allow this healing energy to integrate fully.

4. **Channel to the Physical Plane**: When you're ready to return to your body, visualize the healing energy flowing with you as you re-enter your physical form. Feel the light spreading through your physical body, rejuvenating and balancing your energy.

How to Channel Healing Energy for Others

1.   **Set an Intention to Heal**: Before you project, set the intention to channel healing energy for another person. You can say, "I call upon the highest healing energies in the astral realm to assist [Name] in their healing."

2.   **Visualize the Person in the Astral Realm**: Once in the astral plane, visualize the person you want to heal. See their physical body or energy body before you.

3.   **Direct Healing Light**: Channel healing light from the astral source and direct it toward the person. Imagine the light surrounding their entire body, infusing it with high-vibrational energy that clears blockages and restores balance.

4.   **Focus on Specific Areas**: If the person has a specific ailment or issue, focus the healing light on that part of their body. Visualize the energy flowing into that area and dissolving any energetic blockages or imbalance.

5.   **Seal the Healing**: Once the healing is complete, visualize the person's energy field being sealed with a protective layer of light. This helps to maintain the healing they've received.

Using the Astral Realm to Access Past Life Trauma for Healing

Many physical or emotional issues have roots in unresolved trauma from past lives. The astral realm offers a unique opportunity to access past life memories and heal karmic wounds that may be impacting your current life.

How to Access Past Life Memories in the Astral Realm

1. **Set the Intention to Explore Past Lives**: Before projecting, set a clear intention to access a past life that holds relevant information for your current healing. You might say, "I intend to explore a past life where unresolved trauma is affecting me in this lifetime."

2. **Call Upon Guides for Assistance**: Ask your astral guides to help you access past life memories that are important for your healing. They may guide you to specific places, show you scenes from past lives, or provide you with intuitive insights.

3. **Watch for Flashbacks or Visions**: As you explore the astral realm, you may begin to experience flashbacks or visions of past lives. These memories can come as vivid images, feelings, or scenes that unfold like a movie in your mind. Allow the memories to flow without judgment.

4. **Observe and Reflect**: When past life memories surface, simply observe them. Notice any emotions, people, or situations that arise. These memories often hold the key to understanding current life

patterns, challenges, or traumas.

How to Heal Past Life Trauma in the Astral Plane

1. **Identify the Root Cause**: As you witness past life memories, focus on identifying the root cause of the trauma. This could be an unresolved conflict, betrayal, or emotional wound that hasn't healed across lifetimes.

2. **Bring Healing Light to the Memory**: Once the cause is identified, visualize healing light entering the past life scene. Imagine the energy of forgiveness, compassion, and understanding surrounding the memory, dissolving any negative emotions or energetic ties.

3. **Cut Karmic Ties**: If necessary, perform a karmic cord-cutting ritual in the astral realm. Visualize a cord connecting you to the past life event or person, and imagine cutting it with a sword of light or another tool provided by your guides. Once cut, fill the space with love and healing energy.

4. **Reintegrate the Healed Energy**: After healing the trauma, visualize the reintegration of that aspect of your soul. Imagine that a piece of your soul that had been fragmented or lost due to trauma is now returning to you, whole and healed. Allow this energy to merge with your current self.

In the astral realm, your capacity to heal expands beyond the physical limitations of the material world. By connecting with healing guides and beings of light, visiting energy grids and healing centers, and channeling powerful astral energy, you can transform your healing practice and provide deep, soul-level healing for yourself and others. You also gain access to past life memories and can work to resolve karmic trauma, leading to profound shifts in your current life experience.

Chapter Five: Healing as a Light Worker in the Astral

As a light worker, your purpose is to bring healing, love, and light to others. While this work can be done on the physical plane, the astral realm offers unique opportunities for deeper and more profound healing. In the astral plane, the constraints of the physical world—such as time, space, and the density of matter—do not exist. Here, healing can take place in a more fluid, energetic state, where the root causes of illness, emotional trauma, and energetic blockages can be more easily accessed and transformed.

This chapter will explore why healing in the astral realm is so effective for light workers, how to tap into the universal life force energy available in the astral, techniques for removing energy blockages, and how to perform etheric cord cutting and energy infusion for lasting healing.

Why Healing as a Light Worker in the Astral Realm is Powerful

The astral realm is an energetic dimension that exists beyond the physical, mental, and emotional layers of existence. In this realm, you are not limited by the physical body, allowing you to work directly with energy, spirit, and consciousness. Healing in the astral realm offers several distinct advantages for light workers:

1. Direct Access to the Subtle Bodies

- In the physical world, much of our healing work is focused on addressing symptoms within the physical body. However, many illnesses and imbalances originate in the subtle bodies—such as the emotional, mental, and spiritual layers of our being. The astral realm provides direct access to these subtle layers, allowing you to work at the root cause of issues rather than merely addressing physical symptoms.

- For example, emotional trauma that has been repressed or ignored in the physical world may manifest as physical illness. In the astral, you can directly access and heal these emotional wounds, providing lasting relief for the physical body.

2. Enhanced Connection to Higher Wisdom and Guidance

- In the astral realm, your ability to connect with higher wisdom, spiritual guides, and ascended beings is greatly amplified. These beings can offer insights and healing techniques that are difficult to access on the physical plane. By working with these higher vibrational energies, you can bring in powerful healing for yourself and others.
- Additionally, the astral realm allows you to access the Akashic Records—an energetic archive of all soul experiences. This can be especially helpful in identifying karmic patterns or past life traumas that need to be healed.

3. Freedom from Time and Space Constraints

- One of the most profound aspects of the astral realm is the absence of time and space. As a light worker, this means that you can work on healing across timelines, including past, present, and future. You can heal aspects of yourself or others from past lives, karmic imbalances, or even prevent future illness by addressing energy patterns before they manifest in the physical body.
- Without the limitations of the physical world, healing can occur instantaneously in the astral realm. You can also heal multiple dimensions of a person's being simultaneously, accelerating the healing process.

4. Increased Sensitivity to Energy

- In the physical world, our senses are limited by the density of matter. However, in the astral realm, your sensitivity to energy is heightened. You can more easily detect energetic blockages, imbalances, or disturbances in someone's energy field. This heightened perception allows you to be more precise and effective in your healing work.
- Your intuitive abilities are also amplified in the astral realm, enabling you to receive clear guidance on the best approach for healing each individual.

Tapping into Universal Life Force Energy

One of the most powerful tools available to light workers in the astral realm is the ability to tap into the universal life force energy. This energy, often referred to as **Prana**, **Chi**, or **Source Energy**, is the fundamental life force that flows through all living beings. In the astral realm, this energy is more readily accessible and can be used to heal yourself and others on a deep level.

How to Access Universal Life Force Energy in the Astral Realm

1. **Visualize the Source of Energy**: Once you've projected into the astral plane, imagine a vast, infinite source of light above you. This light is pure, radiant, and represents the universal life force energy. It may appear as a glowing sun, a brilliant star, or a radiant field of light.

2. **Connect to the Source**: Visualize a beam of light extending from this source and entering through the crown of your head. Feel the

energy begin to flow into your astral body, filling you with warmth, light, and vitality.

3. **Absorb the Energy**: Allow this energy to fill every part of your astral body. Visualize it flowing through your chakras, down through your spine, and into every cell of your being. As the energy flows, it clears away any stagnant or blocked energy, rejuvenating your entire system.

4. **Direct the Energy**: Once you've absorbed the universal life force energy, you can direct it toward any area of your body or energy field that needs healing. You can also channel this energy toward others by visualizing it flowing from your hands or heart center into the person you are healing.

5. **Replenish Regularly**: During your astral journeys, make it a habit to replenish your energy field by connecting to the universal life force. This will keep your vibration high and ensure that you have enough energy to heal others without becoming drained.

Removing Energy Blockages: Techniques for the Astral Realm

Energy blockages can prevent the flow of life force energy, leading to illness, emotional distress, and spiritual stagnation. Removing Energy Blockages in the Astral Realm is a powerful practice that allows you to work at the core of energetic imbalances, which often manifest as physical or emotional challenges in the waking world. In the astral plane, energy flows more freely, making it easier to identify and address blockages that disrupt the natural flow of life force energy. These blockages may appear as dense, dark areas, or stagnant pockets of energy within the subtle body or aura.

To remove these blockages, healers can channel high-vibrational light or work with spiritual tools, such as light beams or sacred symbols, provided by astral guides or healing beings. By visualizing the blocked energy dissolving or breaking apart, the healer can restore the natural flow of energy, bringing the individual back into alignment and balance. Often, these blockages are tied to unresolved emotions, past life trauma, or limiting beliefs, so the removal process also involves addressing the root causes behind the blockage. In the astral realm, the absence of time and space constraints allows for rapid and profound healing, and the blockages are not just temporarily relieved but transformed at the deepest level, resulting in lasting energetic harmony.

As a light worker, you can use the following techniques to detect and remove these blockages, restoring the natural flow of energy.

How to Detect Energy Blockages

1. **Scan the Energy Body**: In the astral realm, you can easily scan your own or another person's energy body. Visualize a wave of light moving over the body from head to toe. As this light moves, pay attention to any areas where the light appears to dim, slow down, or feel heavy. These are signs of energy blockages.

2. **Use Your Hands**: In the astral plane, your hands are powerful tools for healing. Slowly pass your hands over your or another's energy body. You may feel tingling, warmth, or a subtle resistance when you encounter a blockage. Trust your intuition to guide you.

3. **Ask for Guidance**: You can also ask your astral guides or higher self to reveal any areas where energy is blocked. They may provide you with visions, feelings, or direct messages that guide you to the specific area that needs attention.

How to Remove Energy Blockages in the Astral Realm

1. **Dissolve with Light**: Once you've identified an energy blockage, visualize a beam of white or golden light descending from the source of universal life force energy. Direct this light to the area of the blockage, imagining it dissolving the dense or stagnant energy. As the light works, see the blockage breaking apart and flowing out of the body.

2. **Use Your Hands to Pull the Energy**: Another technique is to use your hands to manually remove the blockage. Imagine that your hands are pulling the dense energy out of the person's body and into the astral space. Once the blockage is removed, visualize it being dissolved or transmuted by the light.

3. **Replace with Healing Energy**: After removing a blockage, it's important to fill the space with healing energy. Visualize pure, radiant light flowing into the area, restoring balance and harmony. This ensures that no negative energy returns to the cleared space.

4. **Repeat if Necessary**: Some blockages may take more than one session to fully remove, especially if they are tied to deep emotional or karmic issues. Be patient and persistent, trusting the process.

Etheric Cord Cutting for Energetic Cleansing

Etheric cords are energetic attachments that form between people, places, and situations. While some cords are positive, others can drain your energy or cause emotional and spiritual imbalances. In the astral realm, you can perform etheric cord cutting to release unhealthy attachments and restore your energetic sovereignty.

How to Identify Etheric Cords

1. **Visualize the Energy Cords**: In the astral realm, visualize your energy field as a glowing orb of light. Look for any cords or threads that extend out from your energy body and connect to other people, situations, or places. These cords may appear as thin threads or thick ropes, depending on the intensity of the connection.

2. **Sense the Energy of the Cord**: Tune into the energy of the cord. Is it nourishing and loving, or does it feel heavy, draining, or toxic? Unhealthy cords may feel dense, dark, or sticky, while healthy cords will feel light and supportive.

3. **Ask for Guidance**: If you're unsure whether a cord needs to be cut, ask your guides or higher self for clarity. They may show you the impact of the cord on your energy field or provide intuitive insights into the nature of the connection.

How to Perform Etheric Cord Cutting in the Astral Realm

1. **Call Upon Archangel Michael**: Archangel Michael is known for helping with protection and cord cutting. Call upon him by saying, "Archangel Michael, I ask for your assistance in cutting any etheric cords that no longer serve my highest good." Visualize him standing beside you with a sword of light.

2. **Visualize Cutting the Cords**: With Archangel Michael's help, visualize the sword of light cutting through the unhealthy cords attached to your energy body. As each cord is severed, imagine it

dissolving into light, leaving no trace behind.

3. **Release with Love**: As you cut the cords, release the energy of the person, place, or situation with love and compassion. Say, "I release you with love, and I reclaim my energy."

4. **Seal Your Aura**: After the cord cutting, visualize your energy field being sealed with white or golden light. This protective layer ensures that no new cords can form without your conscious consent.

Techniques for Infusing Healing Energy into Physical and Etheric Bodies

After removing energy blockages or cutting etheric cords, it's important to infuse the body with healing energy. This restores balance, enhances vitality, and ensures lasting healing.

How to Infuse Healing Energy into the Body

1. **Channel Healing Light**: In the astral realm, visualize a brilliant beam of healing light descending from Source. Direct this light into your or your client's energy body, focusing on areas that need extra support or regeneration.

2. **Use Your Hands as Healing Tools**: In the astral realm, your hands are powerful conduits for healing. Visualize healing energy flowing from your hands as you place them on the body. Imagine the energy penetrating deeply into the cells, tissues, and organs, restoring balance and harmony.

3.   **Activate the Chakras**: Focus on each chakra, starting at the root and moving up to the crown. Visualize each of the chakras as a spinning wheel of light. As you direct healing energy into each chakra, see it spinning faster and brighter, balancing and activating the entire energy system.

4.   **Seal the Healing**: Once the healing energy has been infused, visualize a layer of protective light surrounding the body. This helps to integrate the healing and prevents any negative energy from re-entering the body.

Healing in the astral realm is an incredibly powerful and transformative practice for light workers. The astral plane allows you to access higher frequencies, work directly with the subtle bodies, and receive guidance from spiritual beings and ascended masters. By tapping into the universal life force energy, removing blockages, cutting etheric cords, and infusing healing energy into the body, you can facilitate deep, lasting healing for yourself and others.

The freedom from physical limitations in the astral realm enables you to work across timelines, heal karmic wounds, and restore balance at the energetic and spiritual levels. As a light worker, the astral realm offers you an expanded toolkit for helping others achieve physical, emotional, and spiritual well-being.

Chapter Six: Healing as a Medical Intuitive in the Astral Realm

As a medical intuitive, your ability to perceive and understand the subtle energies that influence health and well-being sets you apart from traditional healers. You are attuned to the energetic patterns, emotional imprints, and spiritual layers that influence physical health. By working in the astral realm, you can go beyond the limitations of the physical world and gain deeper insights into the root causes of illness and imbalance.

This chapter explores why healing in the astral realm is so effective for medical intuitives, how to conduct astral scans for diagnosis, how to access and work with the subtle bodies, and advanced techniques for diagnosing and treating energetic illnesses. We'll also cover how to enhance your intuitive abilities in the astral to provide more profound and transformative healing for your clients.

Why Healing as a Medical Intuitive in the Astral Realm is Beneficial

The astral realm offers unique advantages for medical intuitives because it allows for a multidimensional approach to health and healing. Here's why working in the astral realm is particularly beneficial for medical intuitives:

1. Access to the Full Spectrum of Subtle Bodies

In the physical realm, medical intuitives primarily work with the etheric body, which is closely tied to the physical body and its health. However, illness and imbalance often begin in the higher subtle bodies, such as the emotional, mental, and spiritual bodies, before manifesting physically. In the astral realm, you have direct access to all layers of the energetic body, enabling you to address the root causes of illness before they become physical symptoms.

- **Etheric Body**: The blueprint of the physical body, containing the energetic structure that supports physical health.
- **Emotional Body**: Stores unresolved emotions, trauma, and feelings that influence mental and physical well-being.
- **Mental Body**: Holds beliefs, thought patterns, and mental conditioning that can affect one's health.
- **Spiritual Body**: Reflects the individual's connection to their higher self and Source, where spiritual misalignment can lead to health issues.

In the astral realm, medical intuitives can work across these different layers, diagnosing and healing at the deepest levels of the human experience.

2. Unrestricted by Physical Limitations

The physical body often presents barriers to fully understanding or treating illness. In the astral realm, those limitations are lifted, allowing you to move beyond the surface symptoms of illness and explore the underlying energetic patterns that contribute to disease.

- **Freedom from the Physical Form**: Without the constraints of the physical body, you can easily perceive the energetic roots of illness, imbalances in the chakra system, or blockages in the energy flow. You can also work on areas of the body that may be too difficult or painful to access in the physical realm.

- **Simultaneous Healing of Multiple Layers**: Healing in the astral allows you to address imbalances on multiple levels (physical, emotional, mental, and spiritual) at once, accelerating the healing process. For example, emotional trauma stored in the emotional body can be released, which in turn alleviates physical symptoms.

3. Enhanced Diagnostic Abilities

In the astral realm, your intuitive senses are heightened, allowing you to detect even the subtlest imbalances in a person's energy field. This heightened perception is crucial for medical intuitives, as it helps you diagnose energetic imbalances long before they manifest in the physical body.

- **Clarity in Energy Patterns**: You can more clearly see, feel, or sense the flow of energy in the body and identify where it is blocked, stagnating, or in excess. These energetic patterns often hold the key to understanding the deeper causes of illness.

- **Ability to Access Past Life Information**: Some illnesses or imbalances stem from unresolved issues in past lives. In the astral realm, you can easily access past life memories or karmic imprints, helping you understand and heal the origins of the imbalance.

4. Deeper Connection to Intuitive Guidance

The astral realm is rich with spiritual guidance from ascended masters, spirit guides, and beings of light who can assist in your healing work. By working in the astral, medical intuitives can tap into this higher wisdom to receive guidance on the best course of healing for each individual.

- **Collaboration with Healing Guides**: You can receive direct messages from guides who provide insights into the person's health, past traumas, or energetic imbalances. They may also guide you in performing healing techniques or offer symbolic visions that provide deeper understanding.

5. The Ability to Prevent Future Illness

In the astral realm, you can detect energetic imbalances and disturbances in the energy body long before they manifest as physical illness. By addressing these imbalances early, medical intuitives can help prevent future illness and maintain overall energetic harmony in the body.

- **Healing at the Energetic Level**: By correcting distortions in the energy body—such as clearing blockages, balancing chakras, and releasing unresolved emotions—you can help your clients maintain a higher state of well-being and help to prevent future health issues from arising.

Conducting Astral Scans for Diagnosis

One of the most powerful techniques available to medical intuitives in the astral realm is the ability to perform astral scans. An astral scan allows you to examine the entire energy body—detecting blockages, imbalances, or disturbances that may be contributing to illness. Below is a step-by-step guide to conducting an astral scan.

How to Conduct an Astral Scan

1. **Set Your Intention**: Before you begin the astral scan, set a clear intention. This might be, "I intend to scan [Name]'s energy body to identify any imbalances or blockages contributing to their illness." Your intention will help guide your intuition and keep you focused.

2. **Visualize the Person in the Astral Realm**: Once in the astral plane, visualize the person's energy body in front of you. You might see them standing, lying down, or as a holographic image. This energy body will represent their etheric body and the layers of their subtle bodies.

3. **Begin the Scan from Head to Toe**: Starting at the crown of the head, slowly move your hands or awareness down the person's energy field. As you do, use your heightened astral senses to feel for any areas of disturbance. This could include areas of heat, cold, tingling, or dense energy.

4. **Pay Attention to Blockages**: Notice any areas where the energy feels blocked, stagnant, or disrupted. Blockages often appear as dark spots, thick areas, or dense energy in the body. These blockages may be caused by unresolved emotions, past trauma, or energetic disturbances.

5. **Ask for Guidance**: As you perform the scan, ask your astral guides for assistance in identifying the root causes of any imbalances you detect. They may provide you with visions, symbols, or intuitive insights about the person's health.

6. **Interpret What You Find**: As you scan, keep an open mind about the information you receive. Sometimes the messages are symbolic rather than literal. For example, you may see images of chains representing emotional bondage or walls symbolizing defense mechanisms. Trust your intuition to interpret the meanings behind these visions.

7. **Document the Results**: After the scan, take note of what you found—whether it's blockages in the chakras, imbalances in the subtle bodies, or specific areas of the physical body that need healing. This will guide the next steps in your healing work.

Accessing the Subtle Bodies for Deeper Healing

The astral realm gives you direct access to the subtle bodies that influence a person's health. These layers include the etheric, emotional, mental, and spiritual bodies. By working within these layers, you can address the underlying causes of physical and emotional imbalances.

How to Work with the Etheric Body

- **Etheric Body Overview**: The etheric body is the energetic blueprint of the physical body. It's closely tied to physical health and serves as the interface between the physical and subtle bodies.

- **Healing the Etheric Body**: During your astral scan, if you notice any disruptions or tears in the etheric body, focus on sending healing light to those areas. Visualize the etheric body being restored to its original blueprint, free of distortions or damage.

How to Work with the Emotional Body

- **Emotional Body Overview**: The emotional body holds unresolved emotions, traumas, and feelings. Emotional wounds often manifest as physical symptoms when left unaddressed.

- **Healing the Emotional Body**: During your astral journey, focus on areas of the emotional body where unresolved trauma or emotions may be stored. You may sense these areas as dense, heavy, or dark. Use healing light or call upon your guides to help release and transmute these trapped emotions.

How to Work with the Mental Body

- **Mental Body Overview**: The mental body contains thoughts, beliefs, and mental conditioning. Negative thought patterns, limiting beliefs, and mental stress can all contribute to physical and emotional imbalances.

- **Healing the Mental Body**: When working with the mental body in the astral realm, identify any negative thought patterns or limiting beliefs that may be causing harm. Use healing light to dissolve these thought forms and replace them with higher, more supportive beliefs.

How to Work with the Spiritual Body

- **Spiritual Body Overview**: The spiritual body reflects an individual's connection to their higher self and Source. When this connection is weakened, a person may experience spiritual crisis, disconnection, or a loss of purpose, which can impact their physical and emotional health.

- **Healing the Spiritual Body**: In the astral realm, strengthen the person's connection to their higher self by focusing on the crown chakra and surrounding the spiritual body with divine light. You may also work with guides or ascended masters to realign the person's spiritual path.

Diagnosing and Treating Energetic Illness

Energetic illnesses are imbalances that originate in the subtle bodies but eventually manifest in the physical body. These can include chronic fatigue, unexplained pain, or emotional distress. In the astral realm, you can diagnose and treat these illnesses by working directly with the energy field.

How to Diagnose Energetic Illness in the Astral

1. **Scan for Energetic Imbalances**: Use the astral scanning technique to identify areas where the energy flow is disrupted. These disruptions often manifest as illness or discomfort in the physical body.

2. **Look for Karmic Patterns**: Some illnesses have karmic origins. Ask your guides to show you any karmic patterns that are contributing to the illness. You may receive visions of past lives or specific events that need to be healed.

3. **Observe Chakra Imbalances**: Each chakra corresponds to a different aspect of physical and emotional health. Scan the chakras to see if any are blocked, overactive, or underactive. These imbalances often point to the root of the illness.

How to Treat Energetic Illness in the Astral

1. **Clear Blockages in the Chakras**: If you find blockages in the chakras, visualize healing light entering the chakra and dissolving the blockage. This restores the natural flow of energy and supports

healing.

2.   **Heal the Root Cause**: Focus on the underlying cause of the illness, whether it's emotional trauma, karmic imprints, or mental patterns. Use healing light, symbols, or mantras to clear the root cause and restore balance.

3.   **Ask for Assistance from Guides**: If the illness is complex or has deep spiritual roots, call upon your guides or ascended beings for assistance. They may provide you with advanced healing techniques or help you access higher-dimensional healing energies.

Enhancing Your Intuitive Abilities for Deeper Healing

Healing in the astral realm requires a high degree of intuitive perception. As you continue working in the astral, your intuitive abilities will naturally expand. However, there are specific practices you can engage in to further develop your intuitive skills.

How to Enhance Your Intuition in the Astral Realm

1.   **Daily Meditation**: Spend time in daily meditation, focusing on quieting your mind and tuning into your inner guidance. This will help you become more attuned to the subtle energies of the astral realm.

2.   **Ask for Symbols and Signs**: During your astral journeys, ask your guides to provide you with symbolic messages related to the person's health. These symbols may appear as colors, animals, objects, or scenes. With practice, you'll learn how to interpret these

symbols accurately.

3. **Trust Your Gut Feelings**: As you perform astral scans or healing, trust your gut feelings or first impressions. Your intuition will often give you immediate insights that may not make logical sense at first but are highly accurate.

4. **Keep a Journal**: After each astral journey, write down your experiences, including any intuitive messages, symbols, or insights you received. Reflecting on these over time will help you strengthen your intuitive abilities.

As a medical intuitive, healing in the astral realm gives you access to deeper layers of the human experience—allowing you to diagnose and treat illness at its root, long before it manifests in the physical body. By working with the subtle bodies, conducting astral scans, and using heightened intuitive perception, you can detect and heal energetic imbalances that influence physical health. The astral realm also allows you to connect with higher wisdom, spiritual guides, and ascended masters who can assist you in providing transformative healing. Through this expanded view, medical intuitives can help clients achieve lasting well-being and prevent future illnesses by addressing imbalances at the source.

Chapter Seven: Protection in the Astral Plane

Protection is a fundamental aspect of astral projection, especially for light workers, medical intuitives, and healers who work with high-vibrational energies. While the astral realm is a vast space filled with opportunities for growth, healing, and learning, it also contains lower vibrational energies and entities. These energies can drain, confuse, or even mislead an unprotected traveler. In this chapter, we'll explore why protection in the astral realm is important, and we'll delve into various techniques you can use to shield yourself, maintain your energy integrity, and stay grounded throughout your journeys.

Why Protection in the Astral Realm is Essential

1. Presence of Lower Vibrational Entities

The astral plane exists as a multi-layered reality, with some layers vibrating at very high frequencies—such as those where spiritual guides, angels, and ascended masters dwell—and others vibrating at lower frequencies, where lost, confused, or negative entities may reside. These lower vibrational entities can attach to your energy field, drain your vitality, or even attempt to create confusion or fear.

- **Entities Feeding on Energy**: Lower vibrational entities often feed on negative emotions, such as fear, anger, or anxiety. If you enter the astral plane unprotected, these entities may attempt to engage with your energy field and drain your life force.

- **Interference in Healing Work**: As a healer or light worker, you're often working with vulnerable clients or sensitive energy fields. Without proper protection, lower vibrational entities could interfere with your healing work, affecting the quality and outcome of the healing session.

2. Energetic Integrity and Sovereignty

In the physical world, we are surrounded by external influences, both positive and negative. These influences become even more pronounced in the astral plane, where energy flows more freely. When you project into the astral realm, your aura and energy body are more open, and without adequate protection, you may absorb energies that don't belong to you or experience energetic interference.

- **Energy Contamination**: Entering the astral realm unprotected can lead to energetic contamination, where your energy field picks up unwanted emotions, thought forms, or even energetic residue from others. This contamination can lower your vibration and interfere with your spiritual and healing work.

- **Loss of Energetic Sovereignty**: Protecting your energy field ensures that you maintain your energetic sovereignty—your ability to control and direct your own energy without outside interference. In the astral realm, maintaining sovereignty is crucial for avoiding unwanted attachments or manipulations.

3. Emotional and Psychological Protection

The experiences you have in the astral realm can profoundly impact your emotions and psyche. Without proper protection, encounters with lower vibrational entities or unsettling experiences can cause emotional distress or lingering fear.

- **Protection from Emotional Drain**: Negative experiences in the astral realm can leave you feeling emotionally drained or fearful. Establishing strong protection ensures that you can explore the astral plane without these negative emotional repercussions.

- **Guarding Against Mental Confusion**: The astral plane can be disorienting for beginners. Lower vibrational entities can create confusion or illusions to lead travelers astray. Maintaining mental clarity and emotional stability requires proper protective measures.

Shielding Yourself from Low Vibrational Entities

Shielding is one of the most basic and effective techniques for protecting yourself in the astral plane. When you create a protective shield, you establish a boundary around your energy field that repels negative energies and lower vibrational entities. This shield acts as an energetic barrier, ensuring that only positive, high-vibrational energies can interact with you.

How to Create an Energetic Shield

1. **Relax and Center Yourself**: Before you begin your astral journey, take a few moments to relax and center yourself. Use deep breathing or grounding techniques (as covered in Chapter Two) to calm your mind and body.

2. **Visualize White Light**: Close your eyes and visualize a brilliant white or golden light above your head. This light represents the highest vibrational energy—pure, divine, and protective.

3. **Build Your Shield**: Imagine this white light slowly descending and forming a bubble or cocoon around your body. See the light expanding and thickening, creating a strong, impenetrable shield around your entire energy field.

4. **Set an Intention**: As you visualize your shield, set a clear intention for protection. You might say, "I am surrounded by the highest light and love, and I am fully protected from any lower vibrational energies." Your intention gives power to your shield, reinforcing its strength.

5. **Maintain the Shield Throughout Your Journey**: Throughout your astral projection, periodically check in with your shield. Visualize it remaining strong and vibrant, repelling any negative energies or entities that may come near. If you feel your shield weakening, visualize reinforcing it with more white or golden light.

6. **Close the Shield After Your Journey**: Once you've returned from the astral realm, take a moment to close your shield. You can visualize it slowly dissolving or returning to the source of divine light. This ensures that you remain protected but not energetically isolated once you're back in the physical world.

Strengthening Your Shield with Color

Different colors have specific protective qualities that can enhance your energetic shield. Here's how you can incorporate color into your protection techniques:

- **White Light**: Represents purity, divine protection, and spiritual clarity. It is ideal for general protection.

- **Golden Light**: Offers high-vibrational protection and is especially powerful for shielding against psychic attacks or negative influences. It also strengthens your connection to the divine.

- **Purple or Violet Light**: Associated with spiritual transformation and the transmutation of negative energies into positive ones. Violet light is particularly effective for dissolving low vibrational energies and maintaining high spiritual vibrations.

- **Blue Light**: Linked to Archangel Michael, the blue light provides strong protection from psychic attacks and shields you from external negativity. It creates a sense of safety and clarity in your energy field.

Using Sacred Geometry and Crystals for Astral Protection

Sacred geometry and crystals are powerful tools that can amplify your energetic protection in the astral realm. Each holds a unique vibration that can strengthen your shield, enhance your focus, and repel lower vibrational entities.

Sacred Geometry for Protection

- **Flower of Life**: This ancient geometric symbol represents the interconnectedness of all life. In the astral realm, it can be used as a protective grid. Visualize the Flower of Life pattern surrounding your energy field, creating a geometric shield of interconnected circles. This grid stabilizes your energy and keeps you connected to divine wisdom.

- **Merkaba**: The Merkaba is a three-dimensional sacred geometry symbol that represents the vehicle of light used for ascension. You can visualize yourself inside a rotating Merkaba (two interlocking tetrahedrons). This rotating field of light acts as a powerful shield, repelling any negative energies and aligning you with higher dimensions.

- **Metatron's Cube**: This sacred geometric pattern contains all the shapes that make up the universe and represents balance, protection, and harmony. Visualize Metatron's Cube around your energy field, forming a protective net of divine symmetry. This symbol brings both protection and alignment with the highest energies.

Using Crystals for Protection in the Astral Realm

Crystals hold specific vibrational frequencies that can assist in protection and grounding during astral projection. Here are some powerful crystals to use for astral protection:

1. **Black Tourmaline**: This crystal is highly protective, grounding, and effective in repelling negative energies. Before your astral journey, hold a piece of black tourmaline in your hand or place it beside you. Visualize the tourmaline's protective energy forming a shield around you.

2. **Amethyst**: Known for its spiritual and psychic protection, amethyst raises your vibration while shielding you from psychic attack. It's also helpful for maintaining clarity and focus during astral travel.

3. **Clear Quartz**: This crystal amplifies your energy field and enhances the power of any protective shields you create. You can program clear quartz with your intention for protection and wear it as a pendant or hold it during your astral journey.

4. **Labradorite**: Known as a stone of transformation and protection, labradorite shields the aura and prevents energy leakage. It's especially useful for healers and light workers who wish to protect

themselves while working with the energy of others.

Invoking Archangels and Spirit Guides for Protection

Calling upon the assistance of archangels and spirit guides can greatly enhance your protection in the astral realm. These beings of light operate at the highest frequencies and can provide strong protective energies to shield you from harm.

How to Invoke Archangel Michael for Protection

1. **Set Your Intention**: Before you begin your astral journey, state your intention to call upon Archangel Michael for protection. You can say something like, "Archangel Michael, I invite you to surround me with your protective light and shield me from any lower vibrational energies during my astral journey."

2. **Visualize His Blue Light**: Archangel Michael is often associated with a brilliant blue light. Visualize this blue light surrounding you, forming a powerful shield that repels any negative entities or energy. You may also visualize Michael's sword of light cutting through any unwanted attachments or cords.

3. **Feel His Presence**: As you call upon Archangel Michael, take a moment to feel his presence. You may sense a warm, comforting energy or feel an increase in your own sense of safety and strength.

4. **Thank Archangel Michael**: At the end of your journey, thank Archangel Michael for his protection and guidance. You can ask him to continue watching over you as you return to your physical body.

Calling Upon Spirit Guides for Protection

1. **Ask Your Guides to Assist You**: Spirit guides are always available to help you on your spiritual journey. Before you enter the astral plane, ask your guides to assist you in maintaining protection. You can say, "I ask my spirit guides to protect and guide me during this astral journey. Please help me stay in alignment with the highest light."

2. **Visualize Your Guides Surrounding You**: Imagine your spirit guides forming a circle of light around you. Their presence helps to create a boundary between you and any lower vibrational entities or energies. Trust that they will protect you throughout your journey.

3. **Communicate with Your Guides**: During your astral journey, you can communicate with your guides if you ever feel uncertain or unsafe. Simply ask them for reassurance or guidance, and they will assist you in navigating any challenges.

How to Return Safely to the Physical Body

Safely returning to your physical body is just as important as protecting yourself during your astral journey. If you've encountered lower vibrational energies or feel disoriented, it's essential to ground yourself and cleanse your energy before fully re-entering your body.

Techniques for Grounding After Astral Travel

1. **Visualize Your Return**: When you're ready to return to your physical body, gently visualize your astral body merging back with your physical form. Imagine the two bodies aligning perfectly, as if your

astral body is gently "clicking" into place within your physical body.

2.   **Take Deep Breaths**: Focus on deep, steady breathing as you reintegrate into your physical body. Feel your breath connecting you to the present moment, grounding your energy back into the physical plane.

3.   **Wiggle Your Toes and Fingers**: Start to move your fingers and toes to bring your awareness fully back into your body. This physical movement helps you reconnect to the sensations of your body and the material world.

4.   **Touch the Earth**: If possible, place your bare feet on the ground, touch a tree, or hold a grounding crystal like black tourmaline or hematite. This will help stabilize your energy and ground you after your astral journey.

Energy Cleansing After Astral Travel

1.   **Smudging**: After returning from the astral realm, use sage, palo santo, or incense to cleanse your aura and energy field. This helps clear away any residual astral energies or attachments that may have come back with you.

2.   **Water Cleansing**: Taking a shower or bath with sea salt can help cleanse and ground your energy. Visualize any residual astral energy being washed away and sent into the Earth.

3.   **Thank Your Guides**: Always thank your guides, angels, or beings of light for their protection and assistance. This gesture reinforces your connection with them and ensures their continued support in future journeys.

Protection is a crucial aspect of astral projection, especially for light workers and medical intuitives. The astral realm contains various energies and entities, some of which may interfere with your work or drain your energy. By employing techniques like energetic shielding, using sacred geometry, working with crystals, and invoking the protection of archangels and spirit guides, you can ensure that your astral journeys remain safe, positive, and aligned with the highest light.

Maintaining your energetic sovereignty and guarding against lower vibrational entities allows you to fully focus on your healing work and spiritual exploration without interference. By taking these protective measures, you can travel confidently in the astral realm, knowing that you are safeguarded by powerful energetic boundaries and divine guidance.

Chapter Eight: Integrating Astral Healing into Daily Life

Astral healing can bring profound transformations and insights, but its true power is realized when you learn how to integrate the energy, wisdom, and experiences you receive in the astral realm into your daily life. Integration ensures that the healing you experience becomes an enduring part of your personal and spiritual growth. In this chapter, we'll explore the importance of grounding after astral travel, how to document and interpret your journeys, and how to apply astral insights and healing for long-term well-being.

The Importance of Grounding After Astral Travel

After an astral journey, especially one where you've engaged in healing work or interacted with higher beings, it's crucial to ground yourself back into the physical world. Astral travel can leave you feeling light, disoriented, or "spacey," which may affect your ability to focus, function, or feel connected to the material world.

Why Grounding is Essential After Astral Travel

1. **Reconnecting with Your Physical Body**: While astral travel is a highly spiritual experience, you live in a physical world that requires your presence and attention. Grounding helps you fully reintegrate with your physical body, ensuring that your awareness and energy are balanced and centered.

2. **Stabilizing Your Energy**: During astral projection, your energy field expands and opens to higher frequencies. Grounding helps condense your energy back into your body, stabilizing your aura and ensuring that you don't become energetically scattered or vul-

nerable to external influences.

3.   **Preventing Disorientation**: Many travelers feel "floaty" or disconnected after returning from the astral realm. Grounding techniques help prevent disorientation, dizziness, or feelings of being unmoored.

4.   **Anchoring Astral Insights**: Grounding ensures that the insights, healing, and guidance you receive in the astral realm can be integrated into your everyday consciousness. It helps you bring the lessons from your astral experiences back into your daily life, where they can be applied for growth and healing.

Grounding Techniques After Astral Travel

1.   **Walk Barefoot on the Earth**: One of the most effective grounding techniques is to physically connect with the Earth. Walk barefoot on grass, dirt, sand, or any natural surface. As you do, imagine roots extending from your feet into the Earth, anchoring your energy into the ground. Feel the Earth's stability and support, pulling you back into your body and the present moment.

2.   **Breathing Exercises**: Deep, rhythmic breathing can help anchor your energy after astral travel. Sit comfortably (or stand) and take slow, deep breaths. With each inhale, imagine yourself drawing in the grounding energy of the Earth. With each exhale, release any disorientation, tension, or unbalanced energy. This practice helps center your mind and body.

3.   **Eat Grounding Foods**: Certain foods can help ground your energy after an astral journey. Focus on eating earthy, nourishing foods

such as root vegetables (carrots, sweet potatoes, beets), whole grains, and proteins. These foods have a dense, grounding energy that helps bring your awareness back to the physical plane.

4. **Hold Grounding Crystals**: Crystals such as black tourmaline, hematite, or smoky quartz have strong grounding properties. Hold these crystals in your hands or place them on your body (such as over your root chakra) while visualizing their energy anchoring you back into your physical form. You can also carry these crystals with you throughout the day to stay grounded.

5. **Water Cleansing**: A salt bath or shower is an excellent way to ground and cleanse your energy after astral travel. As you bathe, imagine the water washing away any residual astral energy and helping you reintegrate into your physical body. You can enhance the effect by adding sea salt or Epsom salts to the bath, which help cleanse your aura and balance your energy.

Documenting and Interpreting Your Astral Journeys

Keeping a record of your astral experiences is essential for integration. Your astral journeys may contain profound insights, symbolic messages, or spiritual guidance that may not be immediately clear. By documenting your experiences, you create a personal record that you can return to, reflect on, and interpret over time.

Why Keeping a Journal is Important

1. **Tracking Your Progress**: Regular journaling allows you to track your progress as an astral traveler. Over time, you'll notice patterns in your experiences, recurring symbols, or consistent messages from guides, all of which provide insight into your personal

growth.

2. **Understanding Astral Symbols**: The astral realm often communicates through symbols, metaphors, or visions that may not make sense at first. Writing these down allows you to interpret their meaning later, especially as you gain more experience in the astral plane.

3. **Integrating Healing**: Healing that takes place in the astral realm may unfold gradually. By documenting your experiences, you can monitor how the healing process manifests in your physical and emotional life, helping you integrate the healing more fully.

4. **Decoding Guidance**: Guides and higher beings often communicate in subtle ways. Journaling allows you to capture these moments of guidance so you can review them and better understand how to apply them to your life.

How to Journal Your Astral Experiences

1. **Start Immediately After Your Journey**: As soon as you return from your astral journey, write down everything you can remember. Details can fade quickly, so it's important to record your thoughts while they're fresh. Even if the experience feels vague or fragmented, write it down. Over time, you'll begin to piece together meaning.

2. **Describe Your Surroundings and Emotions**: Write about where you went, what you saw, and how you felt during the journey. Did you visit a healing center? Did you meet any guides or beings of light? Were there specific colors, symbols, or objects that stood out

to you? Describe the energy of the environment and your emotional responses to it.

3. **Include Sensory Details**: The astral realm can engage all your senses — sight, sound, touch, and even smell. Write about any sensory experiences you had, such as hearing voices, feeling vibrations, or seeing flashes of light. These details often hold clues to the deeper meaning of your journey.

4. **Record Any Messages or Insights**: If you received any direct guidance, intuitive messages, or healing insights, write them down as clearly as you can. These messages may come from guides, higher beings, or simply your own higher self. Even if the message doesn't make sense immediately, recording it will help you decode it later.

5. **Reflect on the Experience**: After documenting the experience, take some time to reflect. What do you think the experience meant? How did it relate to your current life situation, your healing, or your spiritual growth? Reflecting on your experience helps you begin the process of integrating the insights and lessons you've received.

Using Astral Insights to Guide Your Healing Practice

The astral realm is a powerful source of wisdom and guidance. The insights and healing you receive during your astral journeys can be applied not only to your own life but also to your healing practice as a light worker, medical intuitive, or healer. Learning how to incorporate these astral insights into your everyday life will enhance your healing abilities and deepen your connection to your spiritual path.

How to Apply Astral Insights to Your Healing Work

1. **Identify Patterns or Themes**: Over time, you may notice recurring themes in your astral experiences. Perhaps certain symbols, guides, or healing techniques keep appearing. Pay attention to these patterns, as they often hold valuable insights for your healing work. For example, if you frequently encounter specific symbols (such as the lotus flower, a beam of light, or specific colors), these may represent new healing modalities or spiritual tools you can use in your practice.

2. **Bring Healing Techniques from the Astral into the Physical**: During your astral journeys, you may be shown specific healing techniques, symbols, or methods that you can apply in your healing practice. For example, you might learn to work with certain frequencies of light, use new energy healing techniques, or be introduced to ascended masters who specialize in healing. Experiment with these techniques in your physical healing sessions, integrating them into your work with clients.

3. **Use Astral Guidance to Help Clients**: The guidance you receive in the astral realm can provide deep insights into your clients' healing needs. For example, during an astral journey, you may be shown a specific past life that is affecting your client's health, or you may be guided to focus on a particular chakra or energy center. Trust the insights you receive and use them to guide your healing sessions.

4. **Channel Healing Energy from the Astral Realm**: As a light worker or healer, you can bring the high-vibrational energy of the astral realm into your healing sessions. During your astral journeys, you may have connected with powerful healing energies or guides. Visualize these energies flowing through you as you work

with your clients. This allows you to channel astral healing directly into the physical plane.

5.   **Apply Astral Healing to Yourself**: Don't forget to apply the healing energy and insights you receive in the astral realm to your own life. The lessons and healing you experience can be used to enhance your personal well-being, overcome emotional or physical challenges, and continue your spiritual growth. Self-care is essential for healers, and astral healing can be a vital tool for maintaining your own energetic health.

Enhancing Your Empathy and Intuitive Powers

Regular practice of astral projection and healing will naturally enhance your empathy and intuitive abilities. As you become more attuned to the energies of the astral realm, your sensitivity to subtle energies, emotions, and spiritual guidance in the physical world will also increase.

How Astral Healing Enhances Empathy and Intuition

1.   **Heightened Sensitivity to Energy**: The more time you spend in the astral realm, the more sensitive you become to energy in all forms. This heightened sensitivity allows you to pick up on the emotions, needs, and energetic imbalances of others more easily. You'll be able to sense subtle shifts in energy fields, which can greatly enhance your healing work.

2.   **Deeper Connection to Spiritual Guides**: As you work with guides, angels, and beings of light in the astral realm, your connection to the spiritual dimensions will deepen. This enhanced connection makes it easier to receive guidance in your day-to-day life, whether through intuitive nudges, dreams, or direct communication

with your guides.

3. **Improved Emotional Empathy**: Astral healing often involves working with emotions and healing past traumas. As you become more adept at navigating the emotional layers of the astral realm, your capacity for empathy in the physical world will grow. You'll be more in tune with the emotional needs of your clients, and you'll be able to hold space for them in a deeper and more compassionate way.

4. **Trusting Your Intuition**: The astral realm teaches you to trust your intuition and inner knowing. As you continue to practice astral healing, you'll develop a greater sense of confidence in your intuitive abilities, allowing you to trust your guidance more fully in both your healing practice and your everyday life.

Integrating the healing and insights you receive from the astral realm into your daily life is crucial for lasting transformation. Grounding after astral travel ensures that you maintain balance and stability, while documenting your journeys helps you decode and interpret the symbolic messages and guidance you receive. By applying the healing techniques and wisdom gained from the astral realm to your personal life and healing practice, you can deepen your spiritual growth, enhance your intuitive abilities, and provide more profound healing for yourself and others. Regular practice of these techniques will elevate your connection to the astral realm and help you embody the wisdom and healing that you bring back to the physical plane.

Chapter Nine: Advanced Astral Healing Techniques

As you grow more experienced in the astral realm, you will naturally be drawn to more advanced healing techniques that allow you to work on deeper levels of the soul, across timelines, and even with collective consciousness. In this chapter, we will explore a range of advanced astral healing techniques that go beyond individual healing and dive into healing the soul, accessing the Akashic Records, and working with the Earth's energy grid. These practices are powerful tools for both personal and collective healing, offering opportunities to transform the lives of others and uplift humanity as a whole.

Working with Astral Temples of Healing

Astral temples are sacred spaces within the astral realm that are dedicated to healing, spiritual growth, and the transmission of higher wisdom. These temples are often guarded or overseen by spiritual beings or ascended masters, and they can offer immense healing energy, guidance, and initiation into higher levels of consciousness. Visiting these astral temples allows you to receive healing on a soul level and to work with advanced healing techniques.

What are Astral Temples?

Astral temples are high-vibrational spaces in the astral realm that act as centers for healing, learning, and spiritual ascension. They may appear as luminous, ancient structures, sacred geometrical spaces, or light-filled chambers. These temples exist in the higher astral planes, where only beings of light and high-frequency energies reside. Each temple serves a specific purpose—some focus on physical healing, others on emotional or spiritual healing, and some on expanding consciousness and enlightenment.

How to Access Astral Temples of Healing

1. **Set the Intention to Visit a Healing Temple**: Before you begin your astral journey, set a clear intention to visit a healing temple. You can say, "I ask to be guided to a sacred astral temple where I can receive healing for my highest good," or "I intend to access a healing temple to work with advanced healing energies."

2. **Follow Your Intuition**: Once in the astral realm, allow your intuition to guide you. You may feel drawn toward a specific direction, or a guide may appear to lead you to the temple. Trust the process and let the energy of the temple draw you in.

3. **Observe the Appearance of the Temple**: Astral temples often appear as glowing structures made of light, surrounded by protective energies. You might see intricate geometric patterns, sacred symbols, or crystalline architecture. The temple's energy will feel powerful yet peaceful, and you'll immediately sense its sacred nature.

4. **Enter with Reverence**: As you approach the temple, enter with respect and humility. Some temples may have spiritual beings or guardians who guide you inside or perform an energetic cleansing before you enter. Be open and receptive to the energy of the space.

Healing Work in Astral Temples

1. **Receive Healing Energy**: Once inside the temple, you can simply rest and allow the energy of the space to heal you. Imagine yourself lying in the center of the temple, surrounded by beams of light. The temple's energy will flow through your chakras and energy field, clearing blockages, restoring balance, and uplifting your fre-

quency.

2. **Request Specific Healing**: If you're dealing with a particular issue—whether physical, emotional, or spiritual—you can ask the
temple's energy to focus on that area. For example, if you're healing from past trauma, ask the temple to release and transmute any
emotional or energetic blockages tied to that trauma.

3. **Work with Beings of Light**: Many astral temples are inhabited by
beings of light, such as ascended masters, healing angels, or spiritual guides. These beings may offer you direct healing or initiate
you into higher-level healing techniques. Be open to their guidance, and listen for any messages or symbols they provide.

4. **Learn New Healing Modalities**: Astral temples are often centers
for learning, where you can be initiated into advanced healing
techniques. Pay attention to any symbols, tools, or methods shown
to you by the beings in the temple. These may be techniques you
can integrate into your physical healing practice.

Accessing the Akashic Records for Healing Information

The **Akashic Records** are often described as an energetic library or archive that holds the collective memory of all souls, including their past,
present, and potential future experiences. For a medical intuitive or light
worker, the Akashic Records offer a profound resource for understanding
the deeper karmic patterns, soul lessons, and unresolved trauma that may
be contributing to a person's current state of health.

What are the Akashic Records?

The Akashic Records are the vibrational records of all that has ever existed and will exist, often referred to as the "Book of Life." Every soul has its own Akashic Record, which contains information about its journey, including past lives, karma, lessons, and spiritual contracts. Accessing the Akashic Records can help healers identify the root causes of illness, emotional wounds, or spiritual imbalances, especially when they are tied to past life experiences or unresolved karma.

How to Access the Akashic Records in the Astral Realm

1. **Set the Intention to Access the Records**: Before you begin your astral journey, set a strong intention to access the Akashic Records. You might say, "I intend to access the Akashic Records to gain insight into my soul's journey and receive healing," or "I request access to the Akashic Records to understand the karmic patterns affecting [client's name] and how they can be healed."

2. **Visualize a Sacred Library**: Once in the astral realm, visualize yourself approaching a sacred library filled with books, scrolls, or energetic records. The Akashic Records may appear as a vast library, a glowing archive, or a digital space depending on how you interpret them.

3. **Request Permission**: You may encounter a guardian of the Akashic Records, such as an ascended master, librarian, or being of light. Ask this being for permission to access the records. If granted, you will be led to the section of the records that contains the information you need.

4. **View the Records**: Once you're in the records, you may see them
    as books, scrolls, or even holographic images. Focus on the area of
    your life or the person's life that you wish to understand. As you
    explore the records, pay attention to any symbols, images, or intu-
    itive insights that arise. These will often reveal karmic patterns or
    unresolved soul lessons.

Using Akashic Records for Healing

1. **Identify Karmic Patterns**: In the Akashic Records, you may un-
    cover karmic patterns or past life experiences that are influencing
    current health issues. For example, a past life injury or unresolved
    emotional trauma may manifest as physical pain in this lifetime.
    By identifying the root cause, you can work on releasing the ener-
    gy tied to that karmic event.

2. **Clear Old Contracts or Energetic Imprints**: The Akashic
    Records can also reveal old contracts or agreements that may be
    holding you or your client back. These could be vows of poverty,
    loyalty, or self-sacrifice made in past lives that are no longer serv-
    ing you. Once identified, you can consciously dissolve or renegoti-
    ate these contracts.

3. **Heal Soul Fragments**: If you discover that parts of the soul have
    been fragmented or lost due to trauma, you can use the Akashic
    Records to retrieve those soul fragments and reintegrate them into
    the energy body. This process brings a sense of wholeness and
    completion to the soul.

4. **Receive Spiritual Guidance**: The beings in the Akashic Records
    may also provide you with direct guidance on how to heal, evolve,
    and move forward in alignment with your soul's path. This guid-

ance can help you or your client make choices that support long-term health and well-being.

Soul Retrieval: Healing Soul Fragments Lost in Past Lives

Soul retrieval is a shamanic healing practice that involves recovering lost fragments of the soul that have been fractured or displaced due to trauma, grief, or emotional wounds. In the astral realm, soul retrieval becomes even more powerful because the boundaries between time, space, and lifetimes dissolve, making it easier to access and heal these lost parts of the soul.

Why Do Soul Fragments Become Lost?

Throughout our soul's journey, we encounter situations of intense trauma, loss, or emotional pain. In some cases, parts of our soul may fragment and leave the body as a way of protecting us from the overwhelming intensity of these experiences. These soul fragments often carry vital aspects of our energy, creativity, or emotional resilience, and their absence can leave us feeling disconnected, incomplete, or stagnant in life.

How to Perform Soul Retrieval in the Astral Realm

1. **Set the Intention to Retrieve Lost Soul Fragments**: Begin your astral journey with a clear intention. You might say, "I intend to retrieve and heal any lost fragments of my soul," or "I request to be guided to the soul fragments of [client's name] that need to be healed and reintegrated."

2. **Ask Your Guides for Help**: Soul retrieval is a deeply transformative process, so it's helpful to call on your spirit guides or healing guides for assistance. Ask them to lead you to the lost soul frag-

ments or to protect and support the healing process.

3. **Locate the Soul Fragments**: In the astral realm, you may be guided to a past life, a particular traumatic event, or a symbolic location where the lost soul fragments are stored. These fragments may appear as glowing orbs of light, pieces of your own image, or even as parts of your energy body that have been separated from you.

4. **Recover the Fragments**: Once you find the lost fragments, gently gather them into your astral body or energy field. Visualize yourself lovingly holding and nurturing these pieces of your soul, as if you are reclaiming lost parts of yourself.

5. **Reintegrate the Soul Fragments**: After retrieving the fragments, visualize them reintegrating into your physical and energy bodies. Imagine the fragments merging seamlessly with your current self, bringing with them any qualities, strengths, or energies that were lost. Feel yourself becoming more whole and complete as the soul fragments return.

6. **Ground the Healing**: After the soul retrieval, take time to ground yourself and allow the healing to integrate fully. You may experience emotional shifts, dreams, or physical sensations as the reintegrated soul fragments settle into your body.

Healing Collective Trauma and the Earth's Energy Grid

Beyond individual healing, the astral realm offers an opportunity to work with collective consciousness and the Earth's energy grid. As a light worker or medical intuitive, you may feel called to assist in healing global issues, such as environmental damage, social injustice, or collective trauma.

Working in the astral realm allows you to send healing energy to large groups of people, to places of suffering, or to the Earth itself.

Why Heal Collective Trauma?

Humanity is deeply interconnected, and the energy of the collective affects each individual. Collective trauma—whether caused by war, pandemics, natural disasters, or historical oppression—creates energetic imprints that affect the global consciousness. Healing collective trauma helps raise the vibration of the planet, releasing suffering and restoring balance. This, in turn, allows individuals to experience more peace, love, and harmony in their personal lives.

How to Heal Collective Trauma in the Astral Realm

1. **Set the Intention to Heal the Collective**: Before entering the astral realm, set a clear intention to work on collective healing. You can focus on a specific group, event, or situation, or simply state, "I intend to send healing energy to humanity and release collective trauma."

2. **Access the Collective Consciousness**: In the astral realm, the collective consciousness may appear as a vast web of interconnected energies, representing the shared thoughts, emotions, and experiences of all beings. Focus on this web and feel the collective energy flowing through it.

3. **Send Healing Energy**: Visualize yourself channeling high-vibrational healing energy into the collective consciousness. Imagine waves of light or energy radiating out from your heart center, flowing through the web of collective consciousness, and dissolving pain, fear, and suffering. You might focus on specific areas of the world or historical events that hold dense or stagnant energy.

4. **Work with Global Healing Guides**: In the astral realm, you may encounter beings of light, such as ascended masters or spiritual guides, who specialize in global or environmental healing. Ask them to assist in your healing work, and follow their guidance in sending energy where it is most needed.

5. **Visualize Healing the Earth's Energy Grid**: The Earth has its own energy grid, often referred to as ley lines or meridians, that connects sacred sites and carries the planet's life force energy. You can send healing energy to this grid by visualizing it as a network of light surrounding the Earth. Focus on clearing any blockages, restoring balance, and amplifying the flow of positive energy.

Advanced astral healing techniques allow light workers and medical intuitives to move beyond individual healing and engage with higher levels of consciousness and collective healing. By working with astral temples of healing, accessing the Akashic Records, performing soul retrieval, and healing collective trauma, you can facilitate profound transformation and contribute to the upliftment of humanity. These practices expand your capacity to heal not only individuals but also the collective consciousness and the Earth itself, making you a powerful agent of change on a global scale.

Chapter Ten: Ethics of Astral Healing

As a light worker or medical intuitive, your role as a healer in the astral realm carries significant responsibilities. While the astral plane offers boundless opportunities for healing and transformation, it is crucial to operate with integrity, respect, and awareness of the ethical implications of your actions. Healing in the astral realm is a sacred practice, and like any spiritual or healing work, it requires deep respect for the autonomy, free will, and energetic boundaries of others.

This chapter explores the key ethical principles that should guide your astral healing practice, including the importance of obtaining consent, working within the boundaries of free will, aligning with universal laws, and maintaining personal and energetic integrity.

Understanding the Boundaries of Healing Others

Healing, whether in the physical or astral realm, is a profound act of service. However, it is important to recognize that not everyone is ready, open, or willing to receive healing at all times. In the astral realm, where your ability to influence energy is amplified, it becomes even more essential to respect the boundaries of others and ensure that your healing work is aligned with their highest good.

Why Boundaries Matter in Astral Healing

1. **Respecting Autonomy and Free Will**: Every individual has their own spiritual path, lessons, and challenges. It is not your role to interfere with someone's journey unless they have specifically asked for help. In the astral realm, you must honor the autonomy and free will of others, even if you believe that healing is needed. Healing imposed without consent can disrupt a person's growth or create unintended karmic consequences.

2. **Energetic Vulnerability in the Astral**: The astral plane is a sensitive space where individuals' energy fields are more open and vulnerable. This makes it especially important to seek permission before engaging with anyone's energy. Without permission, healing work can feel invasive or disempowering, even if your intentions are pure.

3. **Ensuring Readiness for Healing**: Not everyone is ready to heal at the same time. Sometimes, people need to go through certain experiences or lessons before they are fully open to transformation. By respecting their journey, you allow them the space to come to healing on their own terms, when they are truly ready to integrate the changes that healing brings.

How to Ensure Ethical Healing in the Astral Realm

1. **Obtain Permission Before Healing**: Always seek consent before performing any healing work in the astral realm. If you are working with a client, ask for their explicit permission before beginning the session. In the astral plane, if you encounter someone you feel called to heal, you can ask energetically or telepathically, "Do I have your permission to offer healing?" If you do not receive a clear, affirmative response, do not proceed with the healing.

2. **Respect Energetic Boundaries**: Just as you would respect physical boundaries in the material world, it's important to respect energetic boundaries in the astral realm. Each individual's energy field is sacred, and you should never enter or manipulate someone's energy without their explicit consent.

3. **Offer Healing, Don't Impose It**: In some cases, individuals may decline your offer for healing, even if they are in pain or distress. As a healer, it's important to honor their decision and trust that they are on the path they need to be. You can offer healing energy to the situation as a whole or send loving intentions without directly interfering in their energy field.

4. **Focus on Empowerment, Not Control**: The goal of healing is to empower the individual to take charge of their own healing journey. Avoid any practices that attempt to control or dominate someone's energy. Healing should always support the individual's highest good and their ability to heal themselves.

How to Honor Free Will and Consent

Free will is a fundamental spiritual principle that governs all souls. Each person has the right to make choices about their life, health, and spiritual path. As a healer, you must always honor the free will of others, even if their choices do not align with what you believe to be best for them.

The Importance of Consent in Astral Healing

1. **Consent Protects Autonomy**: Consent is a way of honoring someone's autonomy and their right to choose what happens in their life. In the physical world, this means asking for permission before performing healing work. In the astral realm, this extends to respecting their spiritual boundaries as well.

2. **Healing Without Consent Can Have Unintended Consequences**: Even if your intentions are pure, healing without consent can have unintended energetic consequences. A person may not be ready to heal, or they may have lessons that they need to complete

before they are able to fully accept the healing. If you interfere without consent, you risk disrupting their process or creating imbalances in their energy field.

3. **Energetic Imbalances and Karmic Interference**: Healing without consent can also create karmic entanglements. By overriding someone's free will, even unintentionally, you may take on karma or create energetic debts that need to be balanced in the future. Working with consent ensures that your healing work remains aligned with universal laws.

How to Seek and Honor Consent in the Astral Realm

1. **Ask Permission Before Healing**: In both the physical and astral realms, the simplest way to ensure ethical healing is to ask for permission. For example, you might ask a client, "Do I have your permission to work with your energy field for healing?" In the astral realm, this can be done telepathically or energetically.

2. **Listen to the Response**: If you ask for permission in the astral realm, pay attention to the response you receive. Consent may come in the form of a feeling, an image, or a telepathic "yes" or "no." If you sense resistance or uncertainty, it's important to stop and respect their decision.

3. **Work with Their Higher Self**: In cases where you are unsure of whether someone is ready for healing, you can ask to work with their higher self. Their higher self will guide you on whether it is appropriate to proceed and what form of healing will be most beneficial.

4. **Offer Healing from a Distance**: If you sense that someone may benefit from healing but have not given their consent, you can send healing energy from a distance without directly interfering with their energy field. Simply hold the intention of sending love, light, and healing energy to the situation without forcing it upon them.

Aligning Your Intentions with Universal Laws

Universal laws are the spiritual principles that govern all of creation. They include the laws of free will, karma, cause and effect, and the law of love. When practicing astral healing, it's essential to align your intentions with these universal laws to ensure that your work is in harmony with the greater flow of divine energy.

Key Universal Laws for Astral Healing

1. **The Law of Free Will**: As discussed earlier, the law of free will states that each soul has the right to make its own choices and determine its own path. As a healer, you must respect the free will of others by seeking their consent before engaging in healing and by honoring their right to decline.

2. **The Law of Karma**: Karma refers to the spiritual law of cause and effect, which states that every action has consequences. When you engage in healing work, you must be mindful of the karmic implications of your actions. Healing with pure intentions, aligned with the highest good, helps to generate positive karma. However, healing without consent or imposing your will can create karmic imbalances.

3. **The Law of Love**: The law of love is the highest guiding principle for all healing work. Love is the most powerful healing force in the universe, and when you align your intentions with unconditional

love, your healing work becomes a channel for divine energy. Healing with love means honoring the dignity, sovereignty, and worth of every individual.

4. **The Law of Cause and Effect**: This law reminds us that all actions have a ripple effect. When you engage in healing, be aware of the potential impact of your actions, both in the astral realm and the physical world. Consider the broader implications of your healing work, and ensure that it is aligned with the highest good of all involved.

How to Align with Universal Laws in Your Healing Practice

1. **Set Clear, Loving Intentions**: Before you begin any healing session, whether in the astral realm or the physical world, set a clear intention that your work is aligned with the highest good and rooted in unconditional love. For example, you might say, "I intend to be a clear channel for healing, and I align my work with the highest light, love, and the will of the divine."

2. **Respect Karmic Lessons**: Each soul is on a unique journey, and sometimes illness or suffering is part of a karmic lesson. If you encounter a situation where healing is not appropriate because the person is still learning from their experience, trust that their soul is on the right path. In these cases, your role may be to offer support, compassion, or guidance rather than direct intervention.

3. **Work in Service to the Divine**: Align your healing work with the will of the divine rather than your own personal desires. This means surrendering any attachment to specific outcomes and trusting that the divine intelligence knows what is best for each individual. By aligning your work with the greater flow of divine ener-

gy, you become a conduit for universal healing.

4. **Seek Guidance from Higher Beings**: If you're ever unsure about whether to engage in a particular healing session or how to proceed ethically, seek guidance from higher beings, such as your spirit guides, angels, or ascended masters. These beings operate in alignment with universal laws and can provide insight into the best course of action.

Maintaining Integrity in Your Astral Healing Practice

Integrity is at the heart of ethical healing. As a healer, you are entrusted with the sacred responsibility of working with others' energy fields, emotions, and spiritual paths. Maintaining integrity means being honest, transparent, and accountable in all aspects of your healing practice.

Principles of Integrity in Astral Healing

1. **Be Honest About Your Abilities**: It's important to be honest with yourself and your clients about the scope of your abilities as a healer. If you're uncertain about how to handle a particular issue or feel that you are not the right person to provide healing, communicate this openly. It's better to refer a client to someone else or seek additional guidance than to overextend yourself.

2. **Practice Humility**: Healing is a gift, but it does not make you superior to others. Approach your healing work with humility, recognizing that you are a channel for divine energy rather than the source of healing itself. Humility allows you to remain open to learning, growth, and guidance from higher sources.

3. **Avoid Ego-Based Healing**: Healing from a place of ego, where the goal is to impress others or prove your abilities, can lead to imbalances in both the healer and the recipient. Instead, focus on healing from a place of service, love, and compassion, with the intention of uplifting and empowering others.

4. **Maintain Energetic Boundaries**: As a healer, you must also maintain your own energetic boundaries. This means protecting your energy field, avoiding taking on others' pain or imbalances, and ensuring that your own energy remains clear and balanced. Practice regular energy cleansing and grounding to maintain your energetic integrity.

How to Stay Grounded and Centered as a Healer

1. **Daily Meditation and Grounding**: Begin each day with grounding practices, such as meditation, breathwork, or visualization. This helps you stay centered in your own energy and prevents you from becoming overwhelmed by the energy of others.

2. **Self-Care and Rest**: Healing others can be energetically demanding, so it's essential to prioritize self-care. Make time for rest, relaxation, and activities that recharge your energy field, such as spending time in nature, engaging in creative activities, or practicing yoga.

3. **Regular Energy Cleansing**: After each healing session, cleanse your energy field to release any residual energy you may have picked up. You can use smudging, salt baths, or visualizations to cleanse and restore your energy. This practice helps you stay clear, grounded, and protected.

4. **Seek Support from Other Healers**: Just as you provide healing to others, you may need healing and support from time to time. Seek out trusted healers or spiritual mentors who can offer guidance, healing, and energetic support when needed.

Ethics are a foundational aspect of astral healing. As a light worker or medical intuitive, it's your responsibility to honor the free will, autonomy, and energetic boundaries of others while working in the astral realm. By obtaining consent, aligning your intentions with universal laws, and maintaining integrity in your practice, you ensure that your healing work is in harmony with the highest good. Working ethically not only protects those you heal but also safeguards your own energy, karma, and spiritual growth.

Chapter Eleven: Developing Mastery in Astral Healing

Mastery in astral healing is not a destination, but a continuous journey of learning, practice, and personal growth. As you deepen your experience in the astral realm, you will gain greater confidence in your ability to navigate this multidimensional space, connect with higher beings, and offer profound healing for yourself and others. This chapter explores how to develop consistency in your astral practice, overcome challenges, expand your intuitive and spiritual abilities, and cultivate the mindset and discipline necessary for mastery.

Building Consistency in Astral Travel and Healing

Consistency is key to mastering astral healing. Like any skill, astral projection and healing require regular practice, patience, and dedication. By integrating astral travel into your daily or weekly routine, you will strengthen your ability to enter the astral plane with ease and engage in deeper, more effective healing work.

Why Consistency Matters in Astral Healing

1. **Strengthening Your Astral Skills**: Just as regular meditation strengthens your ability to maintain a calm and focused mind, consistent astral travel practice strengthens your ability to control and direct your consciousness in the astral realm. The more frequently you practice, the more adept you become at entering the astral plane, navigating its dimensions, and working with higher energies.

2. **Deepening Your Connection to Guides and Higher Beings**: Consistent practice allows you to build stronger relationships with your astral guides, angels, and beings of light. Over time, these be-

ings become more attuned to your energy and purpose, allowing you to receive clearer guidance and more powerful healing energy during your journeys.

3. **Enhancing Your Sensitivity to Energy**: The more often you work in the astral realm, the more sensitive you become to subtle energies, both in the astral plane and in the physical world. This heightened sensitivity allows you to detect energetic imbalances, blockages, or disturbances more easily, which improves your effectiveness as a healer.

4. **Overcoming Initial Challenges**: Many beginners face obstacles during their early attempts at astral projection, such as difficulty achieving deep relaxation, fear of the unknown, or inconsistent results. By practicing regularly, you can overcome these challenges and develop greater control over the astral experience.

How to Build a Consistent Astral Healing Practice

1. **Set a Regular Schedule**: Just like any spiritual or physical discipline, consistency comes from routine. Set aside dedicated time for your astral healing practice, whether it's once a day, a few times a week, or on the weekends. The more regular your practice, the stronger your connection to the astral realm will become.

2. **Create a Sacred Space for Astral Work**: Your physical environment plays a significant role in helping you maintain a consistent practice. Create a sacred space that is dedicated to your astral journeys. This space you create should be quiet, peaceful, and free from distractions. Over time, your mind and body will associate this space with spiritual work, making it easier to enter a relaxed

and focused state for astral projection.

3. **Keep a Journal**: Track your progress by keeping a journal of your astral experiences. Write down details about each journey, including the time of day, your emotional and mental state, and any specific techniques you used. Reflect on the experiences and lessons learned after each session. Reviewing your journal over time will help you identify patterns, challenges, and breakthroughs.

4. **Set Clear Intentions**: Before each astral journey, set a clear intention for your practice. This could be as simple as "I intend to heal and strengthen my energy field" or as specific as "I intend to meet my healing guides and learn a new technique." Clear intentions provide focus and purpose for your astral work, making each session more effective and meaningful.

5. **Practice Patience**: Mastery in the astral realm takes time. Be patient with yourself as you practice, and allow yourself to learn from both your successes and challenges. The more relaxed and open you are, the easier it will become to enter the astral plane and experience the healing potential it offers.

Overcoming Challenges in Astral Healing

Like any spiritual practice, astral healing can present challenges along the way. These challenges may manifest as fear, doubt, difficulty entering the astral plane, or obstacles in your healing work. Developing mastery means learning how to navigate these challenges with confidence and resilience.

Common Challenges in Astral Healing

1. **Fear of the Unknown**: For many people, the astral realm can feel
    intimidating or unfamiliar, especially when first starting out. This
    fear may manifest as anxiety during astral projection or a reluc-
    tance to fully separate from the physical body. While some fear is
    natural, it can prevent you from fully exploring the astral plane and
    accessing its healing potential.

2. **Difficulty Achieving Deep Relaxation**: One of the primary barri-
    ers to astral projection is the inability to relax deeply enough to
    separate from the physical body. This may be due to stress, mental
    distractions, or physical discomfort.

3. **Inconsistent Astral Journeys**: Some practitioners experience dif-
    ficulty achieving consistent results with astral projection. You may
    have successful journeys one day but find it challenging to enter
    the astral realm the next. This inconsistency can lead to frustration
    or doubt.

4. **Energetic Exhaustion**: Astral healing can be energetically de-
    manding, especially when working with others or performing in-
    tense healing work. Without proper grounding, protection, and en-
    ergy replenishment, you may feel drained or fatigued after your
    sessions.

How to Overcome These Challenges

1. **Addressing Fear**: If fear arises, remind yourself that you are al-
    ways protected in the astral realm. Before each session, visualize
    yourself surrounded by a shield of white or golden light that keeps
    you safe and secure. You can also call upon your spirit guides, an-

gels, or Archangel Michael for protection and guidance. Over time, the more you practice, the more familiar and comfortable the astral realm will become, reducing your fear.

2. **Enhancing Relaxation**: Deep relaxation is essential for successful astral projection. If you struggle to relax, consider using techniques such as progressive muscle relaxation, breathwork, or guided meditation to calm your mind and body. Creating a peaceful environment with soothing music, candles, or crystals can also enhance relaxation. Consistent practice will help your body and mind become accustomed to entering a deeply relaxed state more easily.

3. **Improving Consistency**: Inconsistent results are often due to fluctuating mental or emotional states. To improve consistency, develop a regular pre-journey ritual that includes grounding, setting intentions, and relaxing your mind and body. This ritual helps to anchor your practice and sets the stage for more consistent experiences. If you have an unsuccessful session, don't get discouraged—each attempt helps you build familiarity with the process.

4. **Managing Energetic Drain**: To avoid energetic exhaustion, make grounding and energy replenishment a regular part of your practice. After each astral healing session, use grounding techniques such as walking barefoot on the Earth, holding grounding crystals (like black tourmaline or hematite), or taking a salt bath to stabilize your energy. Replenish your energy by visualizing light flowing into your body from the Earth or Source energy. Self-care is crucial for maintaining balance.

Expanding Your Healing Abilities

As you continue to practice astral healing, you will notice your abilities expanding over time. This expansion includes developing stronger intuitive powers, greater sensitivity to energy, and a deeper connection to spiritual beings and guides. Mastery in astral healing is not just about perfecting techniques—it's about growing spiritually and energetically as you continue on your path as a healer.

Developing Your Intuition and Psychic Sensitivity

1. **Strengthening Your Clair Senses**: The astral realm heightens your intuitive abilities, particularly your **clair senses**—clairvoyance (clear seeing), clairaudience (clear hearing), clairsentience (clear feeling), and claircognizance (clear knowing). As you practice astral healing, pay attention to how these senses develop. You may start to receive clearer visions, hear messages from guides, or intuitively "know" what needs healing in someone's energy field.

2. **Tuning Into Subtle Energies**: The more you work in the astral realm, the more sensitive you will become to the subtle energies of others. This sensitivity allows you to perceive energetic imbalances, blockages, and emotional wounds with greater clarity. Trust these impressions, even if they are subtle at first. Over time, you will be able to sense energy fields more accurately and make more precise diagnoses in your healing work.

3. **Listening to Your Inner Guidance**: As your intuition deepens, you will become more attuned to your inner guidance or higher self. This guidance often provides insights into your healing work, showing you the most effective techniques or areas to focus on. By listening to and trusting this inner voice, you will become more

confident and adept in your healing practice.

Deepening Your Connection to Spiritual Guides

1. **Building Relationships with Healing Guides**: Over time, you
    will develop deeper relationships with your healing guides, angels,
    or ascended masters in the astral realm. These guides can offer you
    advanced techniques, spiritual wisdom, and direct support during
    your healing sessions. Regular communication with your guides
    strengthens this bond, making your healing work more powerful
    and aligned with higher frequencies.

2. **Receiving Advanced Healing Techniques**: As you gain mastery,
    your guides may teach you new healing techniques that go beyond
    the basics. This could include working with specific frequencies of
    light, using symbols or sacred geometry, or learning how to heal
    across timelines. Be open to receiving this guidance and incorpo-
    rating it into your practice.

3. **Working with Collective Healing**: As your skills grow, you may
    feel called to expand your healing work to include collective heal-
    ing, such as healing the Earth's energy grid, working with ancestral
    healing, or addressing collective trauma. These advanced practices
    allow you to work on a larger scale, contributing to global healing
    and the upliftment of humanity.

Cultivating the Mindset of Mastery

Mastery is not just about technical skill—it's also about developing the
right mindset. A true master is always a student, continuously learning,
growing, and expanding. Cultivating a mindset of humility, openness, and

dedication is essential for reaching higher levels of mastery in astral healing.

Principles of the Mastery Mindset

1. **Humility**: True mastery comes with humility. Recognize that the source of healing does not come from you but through you. You are a channel for divine energy, and it is your responsibility to remain humble and open to continuous learning. Even as you gain confidence in your abilities, remain a lifelong student of the spiritual path.

2. **Dedication and Discipline**: Mastery requires dedication and discipline. Stay committed to your practice, even during times when progress feels slow. The more you invest in your spiritual growth, the deeper your mastery will become.

3. **Embracing Challenges as Lessons**: Every challenge you encounter in the astral realm offers an opportunity for growth. Rather than seeing obstacles as setbacks, view them as lessons that deepen your understanding and abilities. Whether it's overcoming fear, working through energetic resistance, or refining your techniques, challenges are part of the path to mastery.

4. **Alignment with the Highest Good**: As a master in astral healing, your work should always align with the highest good of all. This means acting with integrity, compassion, and love. When your healing work is rooted in service to the greater good, you become a powerful force for transformation in both the astral and physical realms.

Continuous Learning and Growth

Even after years of practice, there is always more to learn in the astral realm. The journey toward mastery is never complete, and each astral journey offers new insights, experiences, and opportunities for growth. Stay open to learning from your guides, fellow healers, and your own inner wisdom as you continue to expand your skills and understanding.

How to Continue Growing as a Master Healer

1. **Engage in Lifelong Learning**: Read books, take courses, or attend workshops on astral projection, energy healing, and spiritual development. Connecting with other healers and spiritual teachers will expose you to new perspectives and techniques that can enhance your practice.

2. **Deepen Your Meditation Practice**: Meditation is one of the most powerful tools for spiritual growth. By deepening your meditation practice, you cultivate inner stillness, clarity, and connection to your higher self. This supports your astral healing practice and enhances your ability to channel higher frequencies of energy.

3. **Collaborate with Other Healers**: Working with other healers or joining healing communities allows you to share knowledge, learn new techniques, and receive support on your journey. Collaboration fosters growth and helps you expand your healing abilities.

4. **Trust in the Evolution of Your Practice**: As you grow spiritually, your healing practice will naturally evolve. Be open to changes in your techniques, the type of healing you offer, or the guides you work with. Trust that this evolution is part of your journey toward mastery.

Developing mastery in astral healing is a lifelong journey that requires consistency, dedication, and openness to growth. By building a regular practice, overcoming challenges, expanding your intuitive and spiritual abilities, and cultivating a mindset of humility and service, you can deepen your connection to the astral realm and offer more powerful healing to yourself and others. Mastery is not about perfection but about continuous learning and alignment with the highest good.

Chapter Twelve: Conclusion and Next Steps

You've journeyed through the foundations of astral healing, explored advanced techniques, learned how to navigate ethical challenges, and have begun mastering the art of healing in the astral realm. But the journey doesn't end here. Mastery in astral healing is not a final destination—it's a lifelong path of spiritual and personal evolution. As you complete this part of your journey, it's time to reflect on what you've learned, integrate your insights into your daily life, and explore the many possibilities that lie ahead.

In this chapter, we will reflect on the significance of astral healing, review the essential lessons covered, and provide guidance on how to move forward in your practice. We'll also discuss the importance of continued learning, expanding your healing work, and finding ways to serve the greater good as you deepen your connection to the astral realm.

Reflecting on the Journey of Astral Healing

As you reach this stage in your practice, it's important to take a moment to reflect on your experiences and growth as a healer. Astral healing is a profound journey that challenges you to go beyond the limitations of the physical world and tap into the vast potential of the spiritual and energetic dimensions.

What You Have Accomplished

1. **Developed a Strong Astral Healing Practice**: Through consistent practice, you've learned how to enter the astral plane, navigate its dimensions, and work with high-frequency energies for healing purposes. You've developed techniques for protecting your energy, accessing higher wisdom, and healing others.

2. **Expanded Your Healing Abilities**: By working with the subtle bodies, energy fields, and spiritual guides in the astral realm, you've enhanced your intuitive and energetic sensitivity. You've expanded your healing toolkit to include powerful astral techniques such as soul retrieval, healing karmic patterns, and working with collective consciousness.

3. **Strengthened Your Connection to the Divine**: As you've progressed in your astral healing practice, your connection to divine energy, higher beings, and universal wisdom has deepened. You've learned to trust in the guidance of your spirit guides, angels, and higher self, aligning your healing work with the greater good.

4. **Embraced Ethical Integrity**: Throughout your journey, you've learned the importance of ethical boundaries in healing, honoring free will, and respecting the spiritual autonomy of others. This foundation of integrity will continue to guide your work as you evolve as a healer.

The Transformational Power of Astral Healing

Astral healing is not just a technique—it's a transformational experience that changes how you view yourself, the universe, and your role as a healer. By accessing higher dimensions and working directly with the energetic templates of individuals, you've experienced the profound power of healing that transcends time, space, and physical limitations.

You've witnessed how healing can take place on multiple levels—physical, emotional, mental, and spiritual—and how the astral realm offers opportunities for soul-level transformation. You've come to understand that healing in the astral is not just about fixing problems but about helping individuals reconnect with their true essence, align with their highest purpose, and realize their potential.

Integrating Astral Healing into Daily Life

While much of your healing work may occur in the astral realm, the lessons and insights you've gained must be integrated into your daily life for lasting transformation. Integration is the process of bringing the spiritual and energetic experiences from the astral plane into your physical reality, allowing you to live more consciously, mindfully, and in alignment with your higher self.

How to Integrate Astral Healing into Your Daily Life

1. **Practice Mindful Awareness**: Mindfulness helps you stay connected to the energetic and spiritual insights gained during astral healing. As you move through your daily life, stay aware of your thoughts, emotions, and energy field. Notice how your experiences in the astral realm have influenced your perspective and respond to situations from a place of calm, compassion, and clarity.

2. **Apply Healing Insights**: The insights you receive during astral journeys can often provide solutions to problems, guidance on life choices, or healing of emotional wounds. Reflect on these insights and find ways to apply them practically. For example, if you received guidance on healing a relationship, take steps in your waking life to repair and nurture that connection.

3. **Maintain Energetic Hygiene**: Regular energy cleansing, grounding, and protection are crucial to maintaining the energetic balance you've cultivated through your astral work. Daily grounding exer-

cises, salt baths, or working with protective crystals will help you stay energetically aligned and avoid absorbing negative energy from your surroundings.

4. **Balance Your Physical and Spiritual Life**: Mastery in astral healing requires balancing your spiritual work with the demands of your physical life. This means staying connected to your body through physical activity, healthy eating, and rest while also prioritizing time for spiritual practice, meditation, and healing.

5. **Express Gratitude and Compassion**: Gratitude is a powerful practice that keeps your vibration high and aligns you with the flow of abundance and healing. Express gratitude daily—for the healing you've received, the guides and beings who assist you, and the opportunities for growth. Similarly, cultivate compassion for yourself and others, recognizing that healing is an ongoing journey.

Continuing Your Path of Growth and Learning

Astral healing is a lifelong journey, and there is always more to learn, explore, and experience. As you continue on this path, remain open to new insights, techniques, and ways of working with energy. The astral realm offers infinite possibilities for growth, and as you deepen your practice, you will discover more layers of healing potential.

Ways to Continue Growing as an Astral Healer

1. **Seek Advanced Training**: If you feel called to expand your knowledge further, consider seeking advanced training in energy healing, spiritual development, or astral travel. Workshops, courses, or mentorships with experienced healers can offer new techniques and perspectives that enrich your practice.

2. **Collaborate with Other Healers**: Connecting with other light workers, medical intuitives, or healers can help you expand your understanding of different healing modalities. Collaboration allows you to share knowledge, learn from others, and combine your strengths to create powerful healing experiences for clients or communities.

3. **Explore New Dimensions of the Astral Realm**: As you gain confidence in your astral healing practice, you may feel drawn to explore different dimensions of the astral plane. For example, you might visit higher planes of consciousness where you can connect with ascended masters or explore ancient spiritual temples for deeper wisdom.

4. **Expand Your Healing Practice to Include Collective Healing**: As you grow as a healer, you may feel called to work on a larger scale, healing collective trauma, societal imbalances, or even the Earth itself. The astral realm allows you to work on the macro level, sending healing energy to places of suffering, natural disasters, or global consciousness. This expands your role as a healer from individual work to planetary service.

5. **Stay Open to Evolving Techniques**: Healing practices evolve as you do. Stay open to receiving new techniques from your guides or developing your own unique methods of astral healing. Trust your intuition as you adapt your practice to meet the changing needs of those you work with, allowing your healing abilities to grow in new and creative ways.

Embracing Your Role as a Light Worker and Healer

As you continue on your path of mastery, embrace your role as a light worker and healer. This role is a sacred calling that requires commitment, integrity, and compassion. You are not just a practitioner of healing techniques—you are a bridge between the physical and spiritual worlds, a channel for divine energy, and a guide for those seeking transformation.

The Responsibility of Being a Healer

1. **Uplift and Empower Others**: Healing is not about fixing others but about empowering them to heal themselves. Your role as a healer is to help others reconnect with their inner strength, wisdom, and divinity. Support them in their journey, offer guidance when needed, but always encourage them to take responsibility for their own healing and growth.

2. **Lead by Example**: As a healer, you are a beacon of light for others. Live your life in alignment with the principles of love, compassion, and service. By embodying these qualities, you inspire others to do the same and contribute to raising the collective vibration of humanity.

3. **Practice Self-Care**: As you give to others, remember to care for yourself. Healing work can be energetically demanding, so make time for rest, rejuvenation, and personal healing. Your own well-being is essential to maintaining the clarity and strength needed to serve others effectively.

4. **Commit to Personal Growth**: Healing is a journey of self-discovery. As you help others, you will continue to learn and grow. Stay curious, humble, and committed to your own spiritual development. The more you evolve, the more effective and powerful your healing work will become.

Next Steps on Your Journey

Now that you've completed this phase of your astral healing journey, it's time to look ahead and set intentions for your next steps. Whether you feel called to deepen your astral practice, explore new dimensions of healing, or begin offering your services to others, trust that the path will continue to unfold in perfect timing.

Practical Steps for Moving Forward

1. **Reflect on Your Goals**: Take time to reflect on where you are in your healing journey and where you'd like to go next. Do you want to work with more clients? Expand your knowledge of advanced healing techniques? Begin teaching others? Clarify your goals and intentions, and set them in motion.

2. **Expand Your Reach**: If you feel ready, consider expanding your healing practice to a broader audience. This might involve offering workshops, creating online content, or collaborating with other healers. Share the wisdom and healing techniques you've gained with those who could benefit from your knowledge.

3. **Create a Vision for the Future**: Visualize what you want your healing work to look like in the future. Do you see yourself working with individuals, communities, or global healing projects? Create a vision that inspires you and aligns with your soul's purpose, and begin taking small steps toward that vision.

4. **Continue to Trust the Process**: The path of a healer is a dynamic and evolving one. Trust in the process and the guidance you receive from your higher self, guides, and the universe. As you follow your intuition and remain open to growth, your healing jour-

ney will continue to unfold in beautiful and unexpected ways.

Final Thoughts

Astral healing is a powerful and transformative practice that offers endless possibilities for growth, healing, and service. As you continue to develop your skills, trust that you are being guided toward your highest purpose as a light worker and healer. Remember to approach each astral journey with humility, openness, and love, knowing that you are contributing to the healing and upliftment of all beings.

The journey doesn't end here—this is just the beginning of an ever-expanding path of spiritual mastery. Embrace your role, trust in your abilities, and continue to explore the vast potential of the astral realm. The more you grow, the more you will be able to share your gifts with the world, creating ripples of healing that extend far beyond yourself.

www.lovelightenergyhealinginc.com

9 7 9 8 8 9 6 6 0 2 4 1 5